REVOLUTION
IS MY NAME

REVOLUTION IS MY NAME

An Egyptian Woman's Diary from Eighteen Days in Tahrir

Mona Prince

Translated by
Samia Mehrez

The American University in Cairo Press
Cairo New York

First published in 2014 by
The American University in Cairo Press
113 Sharia Kasr el Aini, Cairo, Egypt
420 Fifth Avenue, New York, NY 10018
www.aucpress.com

Copyright © 2012 by Mona Prince
First published in Arabic in 2012 as *Ismi Thawra*
Protected under the Berne Convention

English translation copyright © 2014 by Samia Mehrez

Exclusive distribution outside Egypt and North America by I.B.Tauris & Co Ltd., 6 Salem Road, London, W2 4BU

Dar el Kutub No. 2057/14
ISBN 978 977 416 669 3

Dar el Kutub Cataloging-in-Publication Data
Prince, Mona
        Revolution is my Name/Mona Prince.—Cairo: The American University in
    Cairo Press, 2014
        p.   cm.
        ISBN: 978 977 416 669 3
        1. Egypt—History—Protests, 2011—
        962.056

1 2 3 4 5   18 17 16 15 14

Designed by Adam el-Sehemy

Printed in the United Kingdom

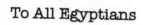

To All Egyptians

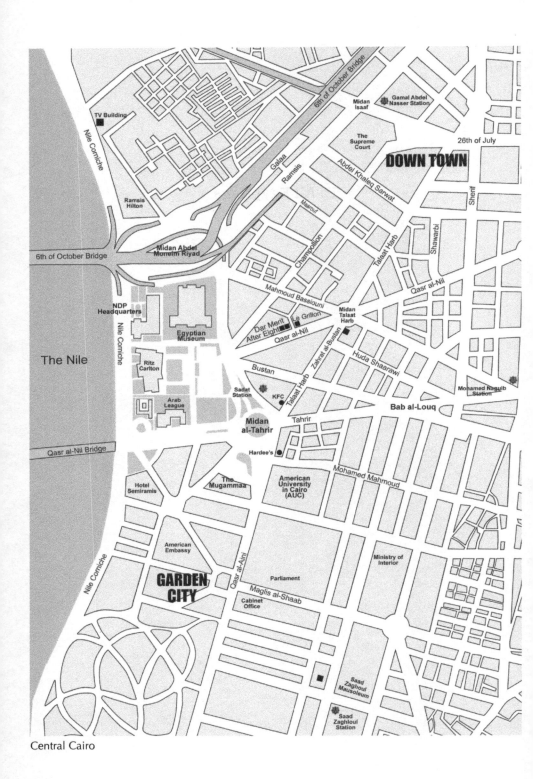

Central Cairo

A Necessary Introduction

"They did it! The Tunisians did it! Bravo! A great lesson for people who want to live and who truly love life—not those obsessed with the Day of Judgment, Hell, and the torture of the grave. Greetings and respect to the people of Tunisia." (Facebook, January 14, 2011)

This was the comment I posted after the Tunisians succeeded in toppling their president.

I called up my friends and relatives, and we congratulated each other as if the Tunisian Revolution was our own. We were sincerely happy for them. I was in my home in Tunis, a small village in the Oasis of Fayoum, following live, and for the first time in my life, a revolution that deposed an Arab dictator. I met up with some of my friends in the village and we celebrated Tunisia's revolution together. And, of course, we wondered whether the Egyptian people would ever rebel. Not in our lifetime.

Next morning's headline in *al-Akhbar*:

"Zein al-Abedin Leaves Tunisia to an Unknown Destination after Increasing Unrest."

There was another headline about Egypt at the top of the page:

"International Organizations: Mubarak has Secured the Highest Levels of Economic Stability for His Country."

I had no comment.

Some Egyptians started to set themselves on fire imitating the young Tunisian Mohammed Bou Azizi whose self-immolation sparked the Tunisian Revolution. A handful died of third-degree burns and the others were rescued. As always in Egypt, we were flooded with jokes:

"Every citizen will be given coupons for one liter of gasoline and matchboxes with his ration card or national ID . . . gasoline is too expensive; make it kerosene instead, because it's cheaper."

"Stop setting yourselves on fire, guys; there will be no one left when the revolution begins."

Again as expected, all those who attempted to set themselves on fire were deemed either crazy or in search of fame. Needless to say, they were considered sinners and would end up in Hell.

I want to quote some of the sarcastic posts about self-immolation that circulated on the Internet:

"Words of Wisdom," as anchor Hamdi Qandil would say.

Member of Parliament Ahmed Ezz: "The solution to the phenomenon of self-immolation is to increase the price of gasoline."

Minister of Finance Boutros Ghali: "New taxes to be imposed on the families of those who attempt to set themselves on fire using gasoline."

Minister of the Environment: "Self-immolation is the cause of the black cloud that lingers over Cairo."

Minister of Labor: "Self-immolation will open up new jobs for the youth to work as firemen."

Prime Minister Ahmed Nazif: "The people don't know what is in their best interest; the proof is their abuse of petro-products."

Minister of Commerce Rashid Mohamed Rashid: "There has been a significant increase in petroleum imports after the rise of self-immolation cases."

Head of the Shura Council Safwat al-Sherif: "Egypt stands above any kind of political blackmail; self-immolators are irresponsible."

TV anchor Tamer Amin: "Self-immolation in Egypt is blind imitation."

The Sheikh of al-Azhar: "Self-immolators are sinners and, as a punishment, should not be rescued."

Minister of Interior Habib al-Adli: "No more than three citizens at a time will be allowed to set themselves on fire in public spaces."

Speaker of Parliament Fathi Surour: "Those in favor of legislation to criminalize self-immolation raise your hand. Motion carried."

al-Ahram newspaper: "Firemen strike and demand a raise after complaints over the increasing number of fires they have to fight."

Political commentator Abdallah Kamal: "Those who set themselves on fire are not Egyptians. They are infiltrators from Hezbollah and they are funded by Iran."

al-Akhbar newspaper: "Egypt imports huge quantities of fire extinguishers."

Secretary of State Hillary Clinton: "The United States demands that citizens be protected against self-immolation and calls upon the Egyptian regime to implement measures that would alleviate popular anger."

Minister of Foreign Affairs, Ahmed Aboul Gheit: "Self-immolation in Egypt is an internal affair. All citizens are free to choose to set themselves on fire."

Barack Obama: "The United States will station its forces in Egypt to protect foreigners and minorities from the smoke caused by fires due to self-immolation."

Hamas: "The phenomenon of self-immolation in Egypt is due to a sense of guilt on the part of Egyptians because of their continuing siege of Gaza."

Prime Minister Benjamin Netanyahu: "We will not return to the negotiating table before Egyptians stop setting themselves on fire."

Ehud Barak: "Self-immolation in Egypt threatens peace and stability in the Middle East."

al-Shorouk newspaper (Algeria): "The Greens are still the best. Algeria beats Egypt in self-immolation cases."

(Facebook, January 20, 2012)

Calls for an Egyptian day of rage began to circulate on Facebook. January 25 was chosen because it was a national holiday in celebration of Police Day. I found out about the event on the "We Are All Khaled Said" Facebook page that I had joined. I had also joined one of their silent flash protests in front of the TV Building on the Nile Corniche during June 2010. I really liked their call for a silent protest where everyone would be dressed in black. I also liked the instructions they had posted on the page to avoid confrontations with the riot police. But the protest in Cairo was not as big as the one in Alexandria and

3

I did not see the crowds of people that had said they would attend the event. Facebook is a virtual space that does not necessarily represent reality, and many people post that they will attend local events when they actually live abroad. I posted that I would participate in the Day of Rage and I shared my status. I liked the idea, but did not believe it would actually materialize: "A Day of Rage in all of Egypt's public squares against injustice, against unemployment, and against poverty—demonstrations that would call for freedom, social justice, and equality."

Here is the status I posted on my Facebook page:

Will we rebel on January 25?
I don't know if we will, but maybe! Over the years, many people have set themselves and their families on fire because of fear, oppression, and hunger, but we have yet to do something about it. We're just good at protesting in the thousands against Denmark because of a silly caricature or because a Christian woman has been abducted . . . . Maybe our euphoria over Tunisia will move us to act. Maybe we won't remain so thick-skinned. Have corruption, bribery, opportunism, passivity, and sexual harassment all become the basic pillars of religion? I don't know. (January 16, 2011)

Most of the comments on my post were actually sarcastic:
"Only one day of revolt?"
"Since when does a revolution have a specific date and time?"
"The most important change we've seen so far is when soccer star Giddou played the last fifteen minutes and scored a goal."
"In Tunisia they called for revolt and people did revolt; in Egypt people just don't get it."
And so on.
The beginning of the year had been disastrous. After the celebrations on New Year's Eve, Egyptians woke up to the bombing of the Church of the Two Saints in Alexandria and the death of tens of people. There were then stories of reciprocal acts of violence between Muslims and Christians, demonstrations in protest and others in solidarity, vigils, and the Orthodox Christmas mass in which Egyptian Muslims

4

participated. If you asked anyone on the street: "Where do you think Egypt is heading?" The answer would have been: "To Hell! The country is burning to the ground."

> It is true that religion is a basic component of the lives of Egyptians but we were Egyptian long before Islam, Christianity, Judaism, or any other religion. If religion will become the cause of our separation and the reason why we kill each other, then we don't need it. And please, don't let anyone tell me that the problem is not with religion but with the people. I'm sick and tired of this refrain. The only solution for this country and for us all is a secular state and a decent system of education. Whoever wants to practice their religious beliefs should do so at home, alone, with their creator. (Facebook, January 4, 2011)

The comments on Facebook sounded more and more like bickering. They were depressing, but I added one of my own: "Life is made up of stages and so, too, is the life of a nation, right? So it's to be expected that Egypt can collapse, disappear from history and geography; that it can be wiped out or simply vanish, right? This has been the fate of many other people like the tribes of Ad and Thamoud in the Qur'an."

Will We Rebel on January 25? I Don't Know

"Egypt Is Not Tunisia." This was the title of a column by Amr al-Shobaki in the daily *Al-Masry Al-Youm* on January 16, 2011. I will quote from it at length:

> Egypt is plagued with a religious craze that has rendered people's demands for fundamental values like freedom and justice or their protest against unemployment and demands for minimum wage highly improbable. Secular, well-educated Tunisia (only ten percent illiteracy) does not have extremist movements like those in Egypt; it does not have new-wave preachers who boast thousands of dispossessed followers and who are responsible for consolidating an unproductive religious "business" that has numbed young people's minds and robbed them of any sense of direction; it does not have a Muslim Brotherhood

that has mobilized tens of thousands of people to defend the Brotherhood's agenda rather than national interests; it does not have religious
orators who have sown ignorance and sectarianism.

A very logical argument indeed, given Egypt's mushrooming problems, particularly during recent years. In addition to this religious
craze and the petty religious decrees that were predominantly about
women, there was also a sexual craze that was clearly manifested in
mob harassment of both veiled and non-veiled women. There was also
the soccer craze that came to the fore during the events that accompanied the infamous match between Egypt and Algeria, as it was all
manipulated both politically and by the media to serve the interests
of the ruling class to the detriment of the interests of an entire people
inside and outside Egypt. All this made me and others wonder: Is
there a state in Egypt? Are there any institutions? Does this country
have a leadership? Does it have any laws? All I could see was orchestrated chaos in all domains that would only lead to Egypt's decline on
all levels in the end.

In the wake of the soccer game between Egypt and Algeria, I had
written the following:

Egypt Is Not Its Ruling Regime
Egypt never was and never will be reduced to the ruling regime and its
cronies. What we are witnessing today is but one of the circles in the
cycle of decline that many ancient civilizations have undergone. How
can one begin to describe a regime that has administered deliberate and
orchestrated popular havoc and has brainwashed the Egyptian people
to the extent that Egypt's very name and reputation lay at the mercy
of the foot of a soccer player who may score or fail to score? How can
we begin to describe a regime that continues to propagate ignorance,
poverty, humiliation, and the killing of the Egyptian people inside and
outside the country for the sake of temporary gains, self-interest, and
hunger for power? How can we begin to describe a regime that is com-
plicit with the Saudi Wahhabi regime that prohibits disobedience to
the ruler, that makes the Saudi kafil a master and the Egyptian worker
a slave, and that describes an unveiled woman who uses perfume or

plucks her eyebrows as a sinner who deserves to be stoned? All of this has led some of our desperate youth to sexually harass girls and women who, according to the Wahhabi doctrine that has saturated Egyptian society with the blessing of the regime, are considered whores. And, by the way, I have never been harassed or hassled in any of those countries that we regularly refer to as 'backward.' Many, many questions.

A Rabid Media Industry

I have no idea how these unprofessional, ignorant, half-literate people ever came to own and run all these television channels. And I don't know who allowed these worthless creatures to ruin not only Egypt's image and reputation in this unprecedented manner but to also ruin that of the Algerian people, their history, and their martyrs to a point that will make it difficult to erase the damage done from both people's collective memory. The media is supposed to inform and teach, not to fabricate events and reality. So what did the Egyptian media, thinking only of immediate gains and not of long-term consequences, do in order to distract people from potentially disruptive issues? It described the soccer game as a "battle," a "war." Indeed, this farcical self-aggrandizing mania went so far as to include broadcasting patriotic songs from the 1973 war against Israel. In addition, the media resorted to lies and the denial of facts aired by other foreign media. The Algerians protested and refuted the fabricated accusations against them. After Egypt lost the game against Algeria in Sudan, the Egyptian media went wild. Like rabid dogs, they pounced upon the bodies of the living Algerians and their dead in successive spats and confrontations of unprecedented abuse, wailing and howling before the eyes and ears of the entire world. The Egyptian media and the regime wronged and humiliated us more than they did the Algerian people. On the same day that Egypt and Algeria played each other in Cairo, Bahrain, Tunisia, and Morocco did not make it into the World Cup, but their media never behaved like ours.

And beyond soccer, what is the Egyptian media good for? Nothing but the propagation of empty slogans, fanaticism, ignorance, and flattery to butter up those who have money but lack any common sense or vision.

January 25: Will There Be a Revolution?
I Still Don't Know

With the escalation of the crisis in the judiciary that erupted during 2006—due to the testimonies of several judges on the widespread fraud of the elections in 2005—I came to believe, as did many other Egyptians, that the country was on the brink of an explosion and that the revolution was surely coming. But the regime had been able to counter and contain the crisis despite several protest movements that emerged: Kefaya, the April 6 Movement, the National Coalition for Change, as well as others. These movements attracted many young people alongside veteran activists and politicians, and had an impact on the street in various parts of the country through calls for public protests and general strikes. Two of the most influential were "Stay Home" on April 6, 2008 and the Mahalla workers' general strike that were both followed by detentions and the torture of protestors by the State Security Forces. Despite this, however, most Egyptians did not want to be subjected to inhuman reprisals by State Security and so didn't participate in these protest movements. It seemed that the only thing that mattered to Egyptians was to put food on the table and to, somehow, have enough money to pay for their children's education. The state had left it up to citizens to resolve their own financial problems, whichever way they could, in other words, through bribery in every sector, whether overt or covert. Egyptians found no problem in calling it halawa, ikramiya, and hasana—a sort of reward or bonus for good work. Most people seemed to be engaged in ripping each other off when it came to the prices of commodities, transportation, public services, and not to mention the widespread swindling that went on in the sale of basic necessities like dairy products, car parts, and so on.

Mohamed ElBaradei appeared on the scene, calling for change and constitutional reform. There was an initiative to collect signatures to form a popular committee of judges, university professors, and public figures to draft a new constitution for the country that would restore Egypt's compromised political and social freedoms. The regime and its media apparatus reacted by conducting a fierce campaign to defame Dr. ElBaradei's public image and reputation. And so this small, newly born spark of hope was quickly extinguished, propelling me and others back to our earlier state of apathy.

This was followed by the murder of young Khaled Said by the police, a case that many Egyptians followed and sympathized with. People started saying that every one of us could be subjected to the same brutality for no legitimate reason and with the sole pretext of enforcing the emergency law. Public protest became a must. The group "We Are All Khaled Said" emerged on Facebook and a campaign was launched to expose the lies propagated by the Ministry of Interior. The number of people who joined the Facebook group increased very rapidly, as did posts for silent vigils and protests in solidarity with Khaled Said that were attended by different age groups and classes and that had no particular political or party affiliations.

Once again, people started talking about oppression, injustice, and the repressive practices by the state against citizens. In fact, those were the only things that reminded you of the actual existence of a state whose institutions had shrunk to one single entity: the Ministry of Interior. With the widening class divide and the rise of poverty, ignorance, and violence, people started to talk about the imminent revolution of the dispossessed: the marginalized sectors of Egyptian society, specifically those from informal residential areas—known as ashwaiyat—would raid affluent neighborhoods and steal from the rich; there would be chaos and blood across the country. The stories published in the media were an omen of what was to come. This was similar to the situation in ancient Egypt during the first transitional period (from the twenty-third to the middle of the twenty-first century BC). Such was the explanation offered by a friend, a specialist in ancient Egyptian history, who had hoped that the president would take the time to read some history in order to rescue the country from its coming fate.

January 25: Will There Be a Revolution? Perhaps

Egypt's modern history tells us nothing about sweeping popular revolutions. We know of a student and middle-class uprising against colonialism in 1919, a military coup in 1952, the 'Intifada of the Thieves' in 1977, the Central Security conscript uprising in 1986, and different workers' strikes. But Egypt's oral history of recent years, as represented by jokes, seems to say something different.

Hosni Mubarak wanted to boost his popularity, so he asked his prime minister to raise prices so that people would complain; then he would cut the prices and people would love him for it. So the prime minister went ahead and increased the prices, but people didn't say a thing. The president was quite perplexed by this, so he said to his prime minister:

"Okay, then, raise income tax to fifty percent."

So the prime minister did as he was told. Still people shook their heads in dismay and kept quiet. The president went crazy. So he said to his prime minister:

"Look, announce any senseless decision that would set the country on fire."

So the prime minister ordered a ten pound toll for every car that used the 6th of October Bridge. People gave a long sigh, shrugged their shoulders, and paid the toll. So the prime minister doubled the toll: ten pounds at the entrance to the bridge and another ten at the exit. People said:

"God help us, what a nuisance!"

And they paid. The situation drove the prime minister nuts, so he issued an order that every person be smacked on the back of the neck after paying the exit toll. The president himself went to witness this development incognito: people would pay the entrance toll, the exit toll, and then get smacked and be on their way. After a while, the president spotted someone who seemed upset and had started to complain. He was pleased and he leaned over and whispered in the man's ear, "What's wrong?"

The man replied, "This is disgusting . . . . I've been stuck here for five hours . . . . This won't do . . . . They have to increase the number of attendants who smack us."

January 25: Revolution!

Nonstop posts on Facebook and the Internet for more than a week.

On January 24 at 6 p.m. I received a number of emails from different friends, all with the same subject: "Share":

Usually, when popular uprisings erupt, the class that rebels is not, in my modest opinion, the one that has access to a DSL connection. I have never heard of revolutionaries who have accounts on Twitter or who have revolutionary meetings through a group on Facebook. What I know for sure is that normally they distribute flyers to incite revolt, but I have never heard of revolutions that are planned on BBM.

To all the owners of broadband and Wi-Fi and Blackberries: Please guys abort this revolution.

Anyone who owns a Playstation or a Wii, an iPad or an iPod or a Mac or anything at all that has an "i" in it: Please guys, just stay home.

To all those who live by the Nile or in a compound or in a villa or even in an apartment in 6th of October City or Rabwa or Safwa or Hafwa: For my sake, take care.

All those who go to Sequoia or eat at Hagg Mori, the sushi man, and those who go to Sangria or the Cairo Jazz Club or Club 35 or Cairo Capital Club, even those who go to al-Shams Club: I beg you not to leave your home on Police Day. You should only do so for New Year's Eve or Valentine's Day, or the Dutch Queen's Birthday: my dears, what have you got to do with all this revolutionary talk?

To our brothers and sisters at the AIS, the CAC, the BISC schools, and to those of AUC, MIU, and MSA—anyone who goes to a school or university with three or four letters in English stuck together for a name—this is not your big day. Leave this one to the guys from the Higher Institute for Cooperation or the Lutfi al-Sayyid Public School. Why don't you just stay put and make it a 'movie night'?

To the guys who use words like "Oh my God," "Bitch," "Duh," "Talk to the Hand," or those who say "I'm going to pee" (in English) instead of "I'm gonna take a piss" (in Arabic): Dude, please stay put.

Anybody who watches *So You Think You Can Dance* or *Dancing with the Stars* or *Glee* or *Grey's Anatomy*: You should know that, on January 25, MBC4 will start airing a *Desperate House Wives* marathon. Don't move, just stay put.

Anyone who knows Hannah Montana or Joey, Chandler, and Rachel, anyone for whom the name 'Mr. Big' is not a shoe store in the down-trodden neighborhood of Waily: Take the Sunday and Monday off and go on a long weekend to Gouna.

Revolutions are ignited by the hungry and the oppressed.

1
Tuesday, January 25, 2011

I am not one of the hungry or the downtrodden, nor do I belong to a political party or a particular intellectual movement. I believe in freedom of expression, but I do not believe that demonstrations that end with violence and detentions are necessarily the solution. I do not have suggestions to change the status quo and I do not see a better or worse future on the horizon. I see a dead end.

I finished grading some of my students' exam booklets that routinely cause me depression because of the mediocre quality of the answers as well as their low intellectual and linguistic levels. But, as one of our deans once told me, students should not be blocked at the university level for more than four years. So, they must succeed and graduate. In other words, I have to pass them no matter what. I kept leafing through the booklets, browsing through the answers, in search of one sentence that might make sense in order to justify the grades I was dishing out left and right. I felt bad because I knew that if I read their answers carefully, most of them would fail.

I looked at the clock; it was almost 1 p.m. According to posts on the "We Are All Khaled Said" Facebook page, the demonstrations would begin at 2 p.m that afternoon. I chose something casual and comfortable to wear and put on walking shoes fit for running, if necessary.

"Mama, I'm going to the demonstration in Shubra."

"Since when do demonstrations take place in Shubra? Aren't they always at the lawyers' and journalists' syndicates in Downtown?"

"Today, they are expected to be in all public squares in Egypt. The demonstrations in Downtown only draw some fifty or sixty people.

They chant for two or three hours, they get surrounded by five thousand riot police conscripts, then they all get beaten up and some get detained. I want to go to Shubra to see what will happen there."

"Okay. Don't be late."

"I'll only be an hour. I have to come back and finish grading."

"Okay. Take care."

Dawaran Shubra

I had never been to Dawaran Shubra before. I called up one of my Christian friends who lived there to ask for directions. He helped me but advised me not to go. I insisted: "No, I'm going."

I took the bus to Shubra. At Midan Ramsis, I noticed a large number of riot police vehicles. I asked the driver to let me know when we got to Dawaran Shubra.

"It's the next stop."

Another young woman behind me asked for the same stop. She got the same answer. I turned around and found a young, veiled woman behind me. She may have been a student or a recent graduate.

"Are you going to the demonstration?"

"Yes."

"How did you find out about the demonstration?"

"There was an event posted on Facebook."

"'Event'? This is not a Mohamed Mounir concert you know. It's a demonstration!"

"I know."

We smiled at each other, and then I asked her, "Are you a member of a political party?"

"No," she replied.

We got off the bus together and walked for a short while until we reached Shubra Street, the area's main artery. A huge billboard in celebration of Police Day had been set up. We took a look around us; nothing looked like there would be a demonstration. A few police officers were standing at street corners; they kept looking at their watches. It was 1:45 p.m. Nearby a woman in her late forties stood alone on the sidewalk. She walked toward one of the officers and began talking to him. I overheard a few words like demonstrations, justice, dignity, and the high costs of living.

"It looks like this woman is here for the demonstration. Let's go and stand with her instead of standing alone."

"Are you here for the demonstration?"

"I have come all the way from Heliopolis behind my husband's back to participate in this demonstration. I parked my car on a nearby street and walked here."

I was a bit surprised, so I asked her, "But why do *you* want to demonstrate?"

"Because the situation in the country has become unbearable!"

The police officers overheard our conversation. They started laughing.

It was now exactly 2 p.m. The first group of demonstrators appeared on the scene. They may have arrived through one of the exits to the metro station across the street. There were around twenty people in the group. You couldn't really call them "youth" since some were in their forties and fifties. They stood side by side with younger men and women. The chants were quite familiar—the same ones I used to hear at the demonstrations during the late eighties:

"People, people come and join us! Brothers and sisters, together, for all of us!"

"Freedom, freedom, come, embrace us! State Security stands between us!"

The older woman and the younger one thrust themselves in the middle of the group and started chanting fervently. I stood nearby and watched.

More groups emerged from the side streets carrying Egyptian flags and banners that read: "Say No to Poverty," "I Want a Job, Big Man," "You Have Stolen Our Daily Bread," "Lentils Cost Ten per Kilo." The riot police conscripts started surrounding the demonstrators and tried to separate them. However, the officers continued to make way for those who wanted to join the demonstration, opening up the area that the policemen had closed off. I moved closer to the center to take photos of the slogans and to better hear the lyrics of the chants:

"What does Mubarak want from us?
People to kiss his feet no less?
No, Mubarak we won't bend!
The people will squash you in the end!"

One of the officers asked me sarcastically, pointing with one hand to the area that had been cordoned off and feeling my arm with the other, "Do you want to join them?"

I looked at him angrily and shouted, "Are you feeling me up?"

He quickly withdrew his hand.

"Okay, no problem. Please walk in."

"I'm not going in," I answered defiantly.

I stood at a safe distance, because I don't like crowds and I don't like shouting, nor do I like vulgar chants or the stench of the riot police who surrounded the demonstrators, pressing against them, so that they would remain on the sidewalk and not occupy the street.

In less than a few minutes, other groups of demonstrators began to appear. The riot police were somewhat at a loss. The different groups succeeded in joining each other; they were now in the hundreds. Some chanted:

"We either get a decent life! Or we will fall in strife!"

I liked the chant, so I started humming it to myself. The riot police closed off Shubra Street on both ends with roadblocks. More riot police began to arrive; they stood side by side, completely blocking the street. I turned around and noticed an officer looking at his watch in exasperation. I smiled at him and said jokingly, "It's still early. We are just getting going."

"But we've been here since this morning."

"Sorry to hear that, but this is your job!"

When the police officer saw that I wasn't joining the demonstrators, he said:

"So, do you support what's happening?"

"I actually don't like demonstrations, but are you happy with your life?"

"No, I'm not. But do you believe that this is the solution?"

"Maybe."

The demonstrators and the riot police conscripts started chasing each other. The police blocked off both ends of the street, so the demonstrators ran to one end and then back again in the opposite direction. This went on for more than a quarter of an hour. Actually, the whole scene was quite funny, not just for me and others like me who were watching, but also for the riot police conscripts themselves, who were laughing despite their visible exhaustion. Maybe it was better to run and move around instead of standing still. I started to move with the crowds; not quite with them, but near them. They were in the middle of the street and I was on the side, near the sidewalk, listening to the protestors calling out to each other from amid the crowds:

"Ya Michael . . . . Ya Adel . . . . Ya Guirguis."

I thought to myself: "Hmmm, the Christians are demonstrating too. Very good! They are on the street despite warnings a day before from all three churches."

I was happy to see two elderly Christian ladies, wearing necklaces adorned with crosses, in the midst of the scurrying demonstrators. We were in Shubra where a high proportion of the population is Christian. Only a few steps away, I saw a large group of demonstrators marching our way. At a distance, I could see my Christian friend. I was delighted and ran toward him and hugged him.

"Where are you coming from?"

"We walked all the way from Tahrir."

"You marched all that distance? And the riot police let you?"

"So far, they've been quite nice."

"What news from Tahrir?"

"People are there in the thousands."

"No way!"

We laughed as we marched along with the crowds.

I was happy that something was happening: I was happy that more than four thousand people from different social classes and different generations were demonstrating in a residential area like Shubra, and that Christians were also on the street. This, in and of itself, was an unprecedented accomplishment.

The tolerant and well-mannered phase of the demonstration quickly came to an end. The police officers had run out of patience. It was hardly 3:30 p.m. when violence erupted.

A group of demonstrators tried to march down Khulousi Street, but were attacked by riot police thugs. They dragged the demonstrators to the ground, beat them, and then arrested them. I took pictures as quickly as I could without a proper focus. One of the thugs saw me. He slammed my arm violently and the camera fell to the ground a few steps away from where I stood. I can't claim that I pushed him away from me, because he was massive, but I think I may have raised my arm in his direction in an unsuccessful attempt to steer clear of his huge body, if only for a couple of seconds. I jumped to grab the camera. He pounced upon me. He hit me in the arm again, even more violently, and the camera fell to the ground again. One of the policemen picked it up and handed it to the "basha," as they routinely referred to the higher ranks of the riot police. It went into one of his trouser pockets. I found myself face to face with a thirty-year-old man wearing civilian clothes and sunglasses.

"Give me the camera, please."

"You won't get it back."

I put my hand inside his pocket and tried to take the camera. He grabbed my hand.

"Let go of my hand. Don't touch me," I shouted.

He let go of my hand.

"I repeat: I want the camera. Who are you to take my camera?"

One of the thugs intervened: "The basha is with the Secret Service."

"Secret Service!" I retorted in visible disgust. "Big deal! I am a university professor. And there's no reason why I should believe that he's with the Secret Service. Show me your ID."

The young basha ignored me. He walked toward the more senior basha and handed him the camera.

"You can go to the basha later and ask him for it."

But before I could start walking toward the so-called basha, the riot police had already started rounding up a number of people and shoving them into small buses. I suddenly realized that the whole scene was being aired live on Al Jazeera. People started chanting and demanding the release of those who had been arrested. The reporter from Al Jazeera had also been detained and it seemed like his arrest was something of an embarrassment to the riot police officers. Before they could do anything about it, a group of young demonstrators had smashed one of the nearby bus windows allowing those inside the bus to jump out.

"Allahu Akbar! We liberated the prisoners!"

I couldn't help laughing despite the drama. I suddenly remembered my camera. So I walked toward the senior basha, who was fuming by then.

"Excuse me, sir."

He walked away from me.

"Sir, excuse me."

He waved dismissively in my direction as if to say, "get lost."

"I want the camera."

I went back to the junior basha.

"I want my camera."

He went off to get it.

"Mind your own business and keep your nose out of ours."

He gave me back the camera. I quickly made sure that it was working and that the photos were still there.

"Merci!"

"And by the way, my wife is a university professor too," he said.

"Really?" I answered, feigning a smile.

The skirmishes between the demonstrators, the riot police, and the state thugs had erupted again. They began throwing stones at each other as demonstrators continued to chant, "Silmiya, silmiya! Peaceful, peaceful!"

By this point, I had had my fill for the day in Shubra and decided to make my way to Tahrir by metro.

Midan al-Tahrir

I struck up a conversation in the metro with a group of young protestors who had been in Shubra. A young man from Alexandria, who worked in Cairo, told us that thousands had taken to the streets in Alexandria. A young Frenchman said he felt very fortunate to be in Cairo during these historic events, especially as he had missed the demonstrations in France that had been taking place for some reason that I can't quite remember. We arrived in Tahrir and joined thousands of people who had succeeded in 'occupying' the midan. I walked toward Qasr al-Aini Street and noticed that there was a lot of water on the ground. It was clear that the riot police had used water cannons to disperse the demonstrators but had failed, given the presence of these multitudes in front of the parliament. Men and women, young and old, even children, with Egyptian flags were chanting:

"State Security, State Security! Where's the state and where's security?"

"Down with, down with Hosni Mubarak!"

I met many of my friends who had started their day in demonstrations that had been taking place in other public squares and who, like me, had ended up in Tahrir. We were all in disbelief that Egyptians had actually taken to the streets. The sight of these multitudes reminded me of the demonstrations of March 19 and 20 2003 against the bombing of Iraq. This time we were on the street for Egypt. But we knew from past experience that the riot police would not allow us to occupy the midan. Young men were being carried on shoulders and were chanting for Egypt, for freedom, for dignity, and for social justice. These were the very same young men who cheered the national soccer teams, al-Ahli and al-Zamalek, and bombarded the rival teams with scathing insults. These were the same young men whom we accused of being immature, with no sense of belonging—a bunch of good-for-nothing thugs. A sheikh, who seemed either to be being carried on someone's shoulders or to be standing on a stage (I could not quite make out given the teeming crowds), started cursing the authorities and their injustices. I didn't mind that. Then he proceeded to holler the all-too-familiar invocation:

"May God grant victory to Islam and to the Muslims."

This really upset me and I began objecting to those who were standing nearby. "Today we are here for Egypt. This shouldn't be turned into a religious occasion."

Some agreed with me while others said, "It's okay. Let him do his thing and then he'll be on this way."

I asked one of the young men to try to make his way through the crowd, to go to the sheikh and tell him that if he insisted on speaking, he should speak about Egypt. But before the young man had made his way to the sheikh, one of the young Ultras started chanting to a drum beat:

"Masr, Masr, Egypt, Egypt!"

Everyone chanted along. That was it! "Egypt!"

From where I stood, I could not see the front rows but it seemed to me that the riot police had started attacking the demonstrators or that, perhaps, the demonstrators were trying to move forward and were being blocked by the police. They began throwing stones at each other but I didn't quite know who had started it: Was it the demonstrators or the State Security thugs—the 'infiltrators' routinely responsible for starting trouble? The truth was that a considerable sector of the Egyptian people had become increasingly violent during recent years—levels of violence I had never witnessed as a child or a young woman. I stepped aside and stood near the Agricultural Development Bank and watched as a number of young demonstrators who had been wounded during the stone-throwing exchange were carried to ambulances parked on a side street. I tried to convince some of the young demonstrators not to throw stones at the riot police, because first, they were protected with visors and shields, second, the stones didn't always fall on them but landed on other demonstrators instead, and third, because we were peaceful demonstrators and not thugs. One of the young demonstrators said that it was the others who had started the stone-throwing and that they were only defending themselves. I felt somewhat lost in the midst of all the scurrying. The demonstrators started chanting:

"Silmiya, silmiya!"

The riot police responded with water cannons followed by teargas canisters. We ran to the midan. We were suffocating, and our eyes were burning and streaming. Some protestors fainted as they were crushed in the middle of the out-of-control crowds. Young women fell to the ground and were quickly carried by young men to the other side of the street. Others rushed a young man in a wheelchair to safety. We moved away from what we thought might be the source of the teargas. I stopped to catch my breath. My nose was burning and my eyes were watery. Someone beside me handed me a handkerchief; another person gave me a can of soda and told me to rinse my face with it. The young Frenchman came running toward me with eyedrops for me and those who were beside me. We barely had time to catch our breath when more canisters were thrown in our direction. This time, the demonstrators caught them in midair with their bare hands and hurled them back at the riot police. As I continued to run, I felt less asphyxiated and the burning became less acute. One gets used to the gas after a while. A young man helped me jump over a roadblock and gave me a bottle of water. I rinsed my face and returned it to him.

"Keep it with you."

"Thank you! That's very kind!"

Meanwhile, the riot police moved toward Qasr al-Aini Street and blocked it, isolating the street from Tahrir. We lost Qasr al-Aini Street to them, so we stayed in Tahrir and looked after each other even though we didn't know one another.

Some young demonstrators started scaling a huge billboard in the midan and began ripping up a life-size image of Hosni Mubarak along with the slogan of the ruling National Democratic Party, the NDP. People started chanting:

"I swear by Egypt, its skies and its lands, this ruin is on NDP hands!"

I liked this play on the lyrics of the popular song by Abdel Halim Hafez, changed to suit the moment. I looked at the shredded Mubarak image on the ground and read the hateful NDP slogan, "For You." I remembered how provoked I used to be when I saw this slogan displayed on billboards on the streets, in public squares, and on flyovers. The slogan was written in classical Arabic, even though half the Egyptian people do not read or write. This slogan had led me to ask on my Facebook page:

"Who is 'You' in the statement 'For You'? Is it Hosni Mubarak or Gamal Mubarak or the people?"

In my opinion, it can't be a reference to the people. If it were, the statement would have been written in colloquial Egyptian Arabic. The more formal, classical version "For You" was just not credible. Demonstrators trampled the torn image of Mubarak with their feet and chanted"

"Down with, down with Hosni Mubarak!"

A young man waved a banner that read, "Red card for the regime."

I strolled around the midan and ran into some of the 'old guard' standing at the edge of the midan: veteran leftists and activists watching, in amazement and in awe, all these young demonstrators who were challenging the riot police, standing unarmed in front of their armored vehicles and water cannons, holding the gas canisters with their bare hands. The faces of the old guard looked different: they were not part of this game. The young demonstrators didn't need their leadership or their wisdom or their theories.

"Game over for you guys . . . . Look at what this young crop is doing," I jokingly said to one of my friends in the group as I shook his hand and kissed him.

He smiled back and waved his hands in a gesture of disbelief.

"They're not like you guys who chant for just half an hour and then go off to Le Grillon for rounds of drinks in the name of struggle."

I heard the call for sunset prayer. Without invitation or prior organization, hundreds of demonstrators from different classes and generations lined up for prayer in the midan. A Tuesday prayer from the heart; one of the most beautiful things I had witnessed that day: this unity, this determination, this profound faith in the face of the power of the police and the regime. The same scene was repeated during evening prayer: Allahu Akbar, God is Great!

Midan al-Tahrir at Night

There was a collective decision to begin a sit-in in the midan. A young man scaled a traffic light in the heart of the midan, another handed him an electric amplifier, and he proceeded to announce the demands of the protestors. If I remember correctly, they were:

1. President Hosni Mubarak and his son Gamal must announce that they will not run for the coming elections later that year.
2. Dissolve the current parliament with its upper and lower houses.
3. End the state of emergency.
4. Release all political detainees.
5. Amend the constitution.

It was as if I were hearing the demands of the 1952 Revolution (or coup d'état) that I had not witnessed. The only difference was that this statement was being announced on an old amplifier, hooked up to a traffic light that was jammed on green, and was being read by one of us in the heart of the midan. Applause, chants, and the national anthem: "Biladi, Biladi."

Suddenly, the chant of the Tunisian revolution erupted in the midan: "The people demand the removal of the regime!"

Just like that! The people demand the removal of the regime. From simple demands that were possible to regime change! This was getting really big! I was torn between feelings of euphoria, pride, amazement, and surprise. Why not just go for it? We had nothing to lose! So I chanted along, as loud as I could and from the depth of my heart.

People were trying to use their cell phones, but the calls were not going through. We started asking each other if the network was working.

"No Mobinil. Vodafone is very weak. Etisalat is erratic."

Someone suggested changing the settings from automatic to manual, but that didn't work either, not even for texting. Others told us that the network was working outside the Tahrir area, so I headed toward Midan Talaat Harb. The phone started to ring. It was my mother.

"Where are you?" she asked briskly.

"I'm in Tahrir," I answered, offhandedly.

"What are you doing in Tahrir? Didn't you say you were going to Shubra?"

My mother's voice got louder, so I moved the phone away from my ear.

"It's getting big, Mama. The demonstrations are for real!"

"What does that mean?"

"It means that we're going to start a sit-in."

"Come home. Enough is enough!" By this point she was screaming, so I moved the phone farther away from my ear.

"Mama, please don't shout like this. You're going to pierce my eardrum! I can't come home. We're in the thousands here, and we're all staying."

"Your father is right here beside me and he says that you must come home. Enough is enough! We don't want problems."

Some of the young protestors turned toward me and smiled. I felt embarrassed.

"Mama, I'm going to spend the night in the midan and I will come home tomorrow. Don't wor . . ."

She hung up on me. I gazed at my phone, feeling quite upset.

One of the demonstrators who had overheard the conversation said to me, "It's okay. My mother did that too."

I shrugged my shoulders and smiled.

Since we were going to spend the night in the midan, I thought I'd go to Bab al-Louq to buy some nuts and potato chips from the store and also get some eyedrops just in case to relieve the burning caused by the teargas. I walked back to the midan through Talat Harb Street since it was the only open access to both the midan and the downtown area.

The riot police had blocked off the other entrance points. I smiled at one of the conscripts who were sitting on the nearby sidewalk and on the steps of the police vehicles.

"You're going to choke on it if you eat it alone," he said.

I extended a handful of the nuts that I had started eating.

"Here, have some, but don't beat us up!" I said, laughing.

"We actually don't want to beat you up, but if we don't, they'll beat us up!"

"Okay, then beat us up softly."

We started laughing together.

I asked them where they were from.

"From everywhere: Sohag, Beni Suef, Asyut, Minya."

"From Upper Egypt? The very best of people!"

"Thanks!"

As we were talking, their meals were being distributed.

"Looks like you're getting a hearty meal!"

"We haven't had a thing to eat since this morning and we've been in this mess since dawn."

"Sorry about that. Eat well, so you can stick it out through the evening with us!"

"What! Are you going to stay until the evening?"

"We're having a sit-in. Come and join us," I answered, laughing aloud.

"Did you hear that, guys? She just said that they're not leaving."

I waved goodbye and headed toward the midan still laughing. I sat with friends on the edge of the stone plinth in the middle of the midan. The garden surrounding it was drenched and muddy because of the torrents of water that the riot police had used earlier against the demonstrators. We shared the nuts and stretched out our legs trying to find comfortable positions. The night would be long and we didn't want to wear ourselves out too quickly. We looked around the midan: Some people were sitting in groups on the ground, others were singing or talking, while others still were resting. Families were strolling about; young people were playing soccer; a man with his very pregnant wife and two excited kids walked by eating nuts. Every once in a while a group would start chanting, "The people demand the removal of the regime!"

Other groups would get excited and join in. My friends and I were quite exhausted (a question of age), so we chanted along without getting up. A middle-aged man with gray hair and modest clothes passed by with a plastic bag full of baladi bread and distributed it among us. "Thank you so much!" We took two loaves and shared them. We looked at each other in disbelief.

"It's incredible that he bought all this bread to give away to people."

Two unveiled young women in their twenties wearing casual clothes were giving out cookies and chocolate.

"Thanks, we've got some."

"Have some more. The night will be long," one of them said, with a charming smile.

"How beautiful!"

We took some and thanked them.

The two women moved on to another group. Two young men came by with a plastic bag full of soda. Again we thanked them saying that we had water.

"Take some Coca-Cola. You don't have to drink it, but you might need it if they use teargas."

So we took two cans just in case.

"Thanks a million!"

How sweet! We had almost forgotten that this kind of solidarity existed among Egyptians. We were also offered tangerines, oranges, and different kinds of sandwiches. In less than half an hour we had food and drink to last us for two nights; from bread all the way to chocolate and cold drinks. We were then given blankets. That was very important since the weather was getting cold and most of us were not dressed for it. We took two blankets, huddled together in a straight line, and covered our legs. Who could have imagined that we would last for the whole day? Who could have imagined that we would actually take to the streets in the first place—that we would be sitting on the ground in the midan among the multitudes that had made this historic day, sharing bread and water? I was suddenly overtaken by a sense of belonging; I felt that I was part of the whole, that my physical presence in the midan was important, and that my voice and my chanting made a difference. Despite the fatigue, I felt an overwhelming peace, quiet, and joy. For the first time ever, I felt that the midan was mine, not just as an individual but as part of the group that had remained in it. I remembered Majida El Roumi's song in the film *Awdat al-Ibn al-Dal* (Return of the Prodigal Son): "The street is ours." Now, the midan is ours. I reminded my friends of the song and we started to sing despite our rusty voices: "The street is ours, ours alone/ All those others are not of us . . . ." Even though I am against the exclusion of others, I still felt that, at that particular moment, that the midan was ours alone.

Two ten-year-olds came by with plastic bags to collect garbage. I was suddenly propelled out of the stupefying ambiance in the midan.

"Where are you kids from?"

"We're from Saft al-Laban."

"Who did you come with?"

"With our parents."

"Bravo! I'm going to collect the garbage with you."

I used one of the plastic bags we had with us, and I started to collect the empty water bottles and cans as well as empty packs of cigarettes. I filled the plastic bag, then I put it by the traffic-police kiosk that had been transformed into a men's restroom and started to look for another bag to fill. Others were doing the same. Everyone was helping to clean the midan. This was something I had never seen in my life! Since when did Egyptians collect the garbage on the street? They had grown used to throwing it out of their car windows, from the bus or the metro, from balconies, in front of buildings, at a passing car, or at the neighbors. I couldn't believe my eyes. I came across one of the street children I knew who hung out in the Downtown area. He always used to hassle me for money. He was crying. I stopped him and asked, "Why are you crying?"

"That kid hit me and took my shoes," he said, pointing at another child at the other end of the street.

"Don't cry. I'll get them back for you."

I went looking for the other kid, but he had disappeared into the thick crowds. I searched my pockets for money and found a couple of pounds. I gave them to the boy I knew.

"Here, get yourself another pair and don't be upset."

To my surprise, he refused the money.

"I don't want money. I want my slippers."

"You always ask for money. Now you don't want it anymore?"

He walked toward his adversary. It was the first time I had seen this! The first time . . . so many things were happening today for the first time. It was the first time for me to be in the midst of thousands of young men without being harassed; it was the first time that Egyptians cleaned their streets; it was the first time that people shared everything they had; it was the first time that people apologized when they brushed against each other unintentionally. I hadn't seen this for such a long time. Was this a different people?

It was almost midnight. I went back to where my friends had been sitting.

"When do you think they're going to start attacking us?"

"At around three or four o'clock in the morning."

"I think they might come earlier. They won't let us stay that long. And tomorrow is a working day."

"Well, we'll just hang out then."

We stretched out and lit cigarettes. A newspaper vendor walked past us. We started to read the headlines of next day's papers. What a joke! The main headline in *al-Ahram* newspaper read: "Widespread Protests in Lebanon." At the bottom of the same page in small font it said: "A Limited Number of Protests Against Price Hikes Have Been Contained." Of course, and here we were, still in the midan. The most daring headline, in red, was in *Al-Masry Al-Youm*: "Warning."

At around 12:30 a.m., I heard the sound of a very peculiar whistle.

"Guys, did you hear the whistle?"

"Yes!"

"Is this the sign that they'll start attacking us?"

We sat up. Ten minutes later, an incredibly fierce attack with teargas began. We left everything and started to run in all directions. Every street we turned into, we were met with tons of teargas and thick white smoke. We didn't know where to go anymore. Canisters and more canisters. They've gone crazy! We ran whichever way we could, bumping into each other along the way. We were blinded and suffocated by the smoke. The bastards were not giving us a chance to find a way out. They were asphyxiating us on all the streets of Downtown and the riot police were hounding us with sticks. I ran toward Merit Publishing House for shelter. The friends who were there were also choking on the gas. The windows were shut where there was a big crowd. Al Jazeera was airing the events live, while Egyptian state channels were broadcasting songs and films. We heard that demonstrators were regrouping in Midan Abdel Moneim Riyad. Some of those present at Merit went to join them. I decided to take a break. I found an empty spot on the floor in the reception area at Merit and sat down. I stretched out and took off my shoes. My feet have been the weakest part of me since childhood.

Later, I ventured out with a friend to take a look around. We avoided the main streets. Before we got to Ramsis Street, coming from Maarouf Street, we heard the sound of shots.

"Did you hear that?"

"It's the canisters."

"No, that's not the sound of canisters. I know what they sound like. Here it goes again. Listen."

"It's the canisters I tell you."

"No it's not!"

We stood near the sidewalk adjacent to the exit of the 6th of October Bridge. We listened carefully.

"That's the sound of bullets."

A group of young people started running toward us.

"Don't go there. They're shooting at anyone who comes near the NDP headquarters with live bullets."

"Damn! Has it come to live bullets?"

We were nailed to the ground as we overheard more shooting. A man and a woman in a car drove by. A cross was hanging from the front mirror inside the car.

"Where are you going?" the man asked.

"Nowhere in particular," I answered distractedly.

"Please get in. We'll take you away from here. It's very dangerous," the woman said.

"Thanks, but we live in Downtown."

The man waved goodbye and they took off. I shook my head in disbelief.

"I've never seen this before! A man and his wife in their car stop to ask strangers where they're going and offer them a lift."

"That's Egyptians in hard times for you."

"And why can't we be like this all the time?"

"What a time to argue . . . so very Egyptian of you."

I laughed, even though it really wasn't the right time to be laughing.

"Okay, let's go back to Merit."

"I'm going home."

"Lucky you! You live just a couple of steps away."

We parted on Qasr al-Nil Street in front of Le Grillon. I started to walk toward Merit, but before I had reached the building, I heard a car come to a brisk stop. I cautiously turned around. There were two relatively new cars parked in front of the club After Eight. A man and a boy got out of one of the cars; the man started smashing the glass façade of a cigarette vendor's kiosk and the cooler right next to it. The boy grabbed stuff from the kiosk and handed it to the people in the other car. I was astonished and couldn't quite understand what was happening. The man sensed my presence and signaled to the person in the car. I stepped back a little.

"We're just grabbing some cookies," he said.

I didn't know what to do. The two cars took off, driving against the one-way traffic. I went to Merit and reported what I had seen.

"They can't be thieves. Stealing cookies in a car?"

"They might be State Security or police."

"They go around smashing up shops and then they accuse the demonstrators."

"But the guys who broke into Drinkies store in Mohandesin were not thieves. They were cool!"

"What happened in Mohandesin?"

"Some really cool guys who were at the demonstration went into Drinkies, cleaned out the liquor, and brought out the beer cooler on the street, but they didn't steal it. They shared it and drank it on the street."

"It was really cool! They were selling a can of beer for one pound. Those who didn't have the money could drink for free."

"No way! Too bad we weren't at that demonstration."

I got home by dawn. I crept quietly into my room so as not to wake my parents and to avoid having to listen to all kinds of things that would ruin the bliss of this historic day. Now, I was certain that we would continue demonstrating and being on the streets. It was not going to be one day of rage but many. Those who were not on the street on January 25 missed out on half their lives.

2
Wednesday, January 26, 2011

Morning: Facebook Session

"Greetings to the Egyptian youth who proved that they deserve respect. My apologies for having doubted them, for having under-estimated their sense of awareness, and for having accused them of ignorance and shallowness. They don't have to be PhD holders in order to be informed and to be active. I'm sorry, truly sorry. Bravo! You have done what we failed to do when we were your age. But we must continue. And guys, please don't throw the stones back at the police because they fall on us and we're the ones who get hurt. Let's look after each other. Yes, we can . . . . Yes, we will."

I received a message from a friend on Facebook from Algeria whom I did not know in person. She had been following events in Tunisia and now in Egypt. "Please circulate this information: In order to stop the effect of the teargas canister, put it in a bowl of water for a couple of seconds. Please let people know. Also use a dampened cloth with vin-egar to cover your nose."

The TV had been on all morning. My parents were watching the news, flipping through different channels. Protests continued in sev-eral cities in Egypt. My father anxiously gripped the remote control; my mother was chopping vegetables with her eyes glued to the screen so that she accidentally hurt her finger. I got ready to go. My mother turned to me.

"Where do you think you're going?"

"I'm going to Downtown."

"Looking for another demonstration? After what happened yesterday?"

I shrugged my shoulders and did not answer.

"Do you like what your daughter is doing?"

My father shrugged his shoulders too and did not answer.

"Your silence is precisely what encourages her. Anyway, before you go anywhere, go get me my prescription from al-Raai al-Saleh Clinic."

"Sure."

"Take good care of yourself, and call to let us know you are well," said my father.

"I will, Baba. Pray for us."

"I've been praying for you all day since yesterday. God protect you. You are the only hope for this country."

"Thank you, Baba. You're the best!"

"Get me the medication first, you hear? And don't lose it!"

"Yes, Mama."

Afternoon

I made my way toward Downtown. There was a group of demonstrators chanting in front of the Supreme Court, like the day before. There were police officers everywhere and tens of riot police vehicles. I was tempted to join the protestors but decided that I should first get the prescription and then join them. I hurried toward al-Raai al-Saleh Clinic; I sat and waited for my turn. The nurse called out my mother's name, so I jumped into the doctor's office.

"Good evening, Doctor."

"Good evening. Please have a seat."

The doctor looked at me intently.

"Were you at the demonstrations yesterday?"

"Yes," I answered with a smile.

"I saw you on television."

"I'm going again now—to the demonstration in Midan Isaaf."

"You're not going to get anywhere," said the nurse as he completed the information sheet."

I turned in his direction. I had never before seen such gloom personified.

"Why do you say that? Had you been there yesterday, you would have seen that there is hope, a lot of hope. This time it's different."

"I actually want to die," the nurse said, without lifting his gaze from the paperwork.

I put my hand on his shoulder and said, "That's why we were on the street yesterday. And we'll be there again today and tomorrow so that you don't have to say that again."

"And why shouldn't I say this? We were created to die at the end."

"No, we were not created to die. We were created to live and to live well and to have fun."

"But at the end, we will still die."

"Okay, but let's live first. Believe me, if you join us, you will change your mind and you won't be so pessimistic."

The doctor had finished writing the prescription. He handed it to me with a smile.

"God be with you."

"Thanks, but God will only be with us if we move and act. God will not change a people if they do not change themselves. Right?" I said, laughing.

"This one is meant for you," the doctor said, addressing the nurse.

"Empty words."

"God help us! You're a hopeless case!"

"Thank you, Doctor. Have a good day."

"Goodbye."

I walked out of the clinic feeling quite shocked. I couldn't believe how desperate and hopeless the nurse was. God knows what he's been through, I said to myself.

I went back to Isaaf. Hundreds of demonstrators had blocked Ramsis Street. There were government employees, students, and workers. The employees of the Mugammaa were following the scene from the windows; some were chanting along:

"Ya Gamal, tell your dad, the Egyptian people hate you bad!"

"Leave! Go! Like Farouk, ho!"

I joined the demonstrators, but my voice was in no shape for chanting. I made my way among the crowds and was surprised to see five young women who looked alike leading the chanting in the front row. They may have been sisters or relatives. The riot police vehicles were double-parked throughout the street, in endlessly lines. The demonstrators had occupied the intersection between Ramsis and 26th of July streets. The riot police had blocked the traffic on the Maarouf Street exit from the October Bridge. The Galaa Street exit was open. The chanting grew louder:

"Revolution, revolution, till victory! Revolution in all the streets of the country!"

"Revolution in Tunisia! Revolution in Egypt!"

The riot police began to surround us as we chanted. They were waiting for imminent orders to start beating us up. The chants changed and grew louder as the riot police closed in:

"The people demand the removal of the regime!"

"Leave! Go!"

I looked at the conscripts; some turned their gaze away, refusing to look us in the eye, others felt uneasy, while others still were moving their lips and chanting along silently, "The people demand the removal of the regime." The officers were on their walkie-talkies. It looked like we were going to get beaten up. I stepped out of the crowd and stood to the side. I didn't want to be trampled by the demonstrators.

Suddenly, the riot police attacked us with their sticks. I intuitively jumped over the green steel barrier. I looked behind me: The five girls had fallen to the ground. Young men and boys quickly helped them to their feet and began running. The police ran after them. I saw some of the policemen waving their sticks in midair, as if threatening to bash people's heads. The demonstrators dispersed, some ran toward Bulaq Aboul Ela.

I stood on the sidewalk behind the barrier angrily eyeing the officers.

"Get out of here."

"How very manly! Pushing girls to the ground!"

"Get out of here, for your own good."

I walked away toward Tahrir. I found another demonstration in front of the Lawyers' Syndicate that was surrounded by riot police. The demonstrators were older and would not survive a confrontation with the police; they wouldn't even be able to run. I stood and watched for a while. I saw an armored vehicle turn around in Abdel

Khaleq Street so as to block Ramsis Street and face the demonstrators. I overheard a young man say, "Look, they're going to hose them with water. Those sons of . . . ."

I looked at him and his friend; they were really shady. These are the kids I'm scared to come near. I put my hand on the young man's shoulder and gently said, "Please don't swear."

The young man was taken by surprise.

"I'm sorry," he said, laughing. "But can't you see what they're doing?"

"Yes, I can see, but that doesn't mean that I have to hear swearing on the street."

"Okay, sorry. Don't use dirty words again, man," his friend said. He then looked at me and asked, "Weren't you in Tahrir yesterday?"

"Yes."

"So were we! We were there until they started beating us up, and then we went to Abdel Moneim Riyad where they beat us up again, then we walked to Shubra. We woke people up and continued the demonstration until dawn."

"Bravo!"

We shook hands and I headed toward Tahrir. An officer stopped me at the corner of Champollion Street.

"You can't go through."

"Since when?"

"That's an order. If you try, you'll be arrested."

"Shame on you. Didn't you have enough yesterday?"

"Get out of here, for your own sake."

"I'm impressed! How very manly!"

"Manly indeed! Do you want me to show you?"

"More than what I've already seen?"

I went into Champollion Street and continued on to Qasr al-Nil to get to Merit.

Evening

We heard that there was a demonstration in Downtown. My friends and I left Zahrat al-Bustan coffeehouse to join it. This was a very youthful and determined group of demonstrators who marched from one street to another. We joined other demonstrators on Qasr al-Nil Street near Midan Talaat Harb. The young men and women were chanting like soccer fans in a stadium:

"Leave! Go! Ho, ho!"

We, the older crowd, were moved to chant along with them. We made our way amid the cars without obstructing traffic. Some rolled down their windows and greeted us, while others kept them shut and eyed us with disgust. We marched into Shawarbi Street. The young demonstrators were marching at a fast pace so that we almost had to run to catch up with them, while the riot police were fast behind us. I overheard them talking on their walkie-talkies. They just didn't know how to encircle us.

They were damn quick.

We continued on to Abdel Khaleq Sarwat Street and then on to Sherif Street. More young men and women joined us. We saw more riot police and the chanting grew louder. They began attacking the front-lines of the demonstration at 26th of July Street, as well as the back rows at Sherif Street. We started to run as fast as we could. I crossed over to the sidewalk to seek shelter inside one of the shops. The nearby shops had shut down and the owners stood by watching. State Security thugs in plain clothes started dragging the young men and women across the ground. They arrested and beat them violently. I saw them capture a young man who had been walking in front of me, chanting and clapping just like me. They beat and kicked him, then pushed him to the ground near one of the shops and continued to kick and swear at him. I started screaming for help but no one moved. I yelled at the thugs, "Enough! Have mercy. You are inhuman. What are you?"

A woman in a black cloak emerged.

"Don't yell at the men like that. No manners!"

"Men? What men? Can't you see what they're doing?"

"You still shouldn't behave like this."

"I can't believe you! They're going to kill the boy. You should be blaming them instead of blaming me."

"This is between men. Women should stay out of it."

I yelled at them as loud as I could.

"You are animals."

"Get her!"

I had barely even finished my sentence when three huge men pounced on me and, before I had time to realize what was happening, one was pulling my hair, another was slapping me, and a third was swearing at me. They beat and kicked me and continued to swear at me using filthy words I had never heard before. I did not scream despite the suddenness of the assault. I would not have been able to scream since one of them had placed his heavy hand on my mouth. My mind raced: Should I bite his hand? It would be difficult. Should I kick him in his crotch? But before I could move, they had hurled me to the ground next to the young man who had passed out by then. I lay sprawled next to him, face to the ground with their boots still over my head. I spat out the blood that had gushed into my mouth. I surrendered my body to them. My glasses had been bent. Anything but my glasses! I had to protect them. I quietly took them off and placed them in the corner at the entrance to the shop. They continued to kick my back and sides while showering me with insults for no reason other than sheer rage and deliberate humiliation. They pulled me by the hair. I quickly put on my glasses. They were dragging me along the street. I tried to grip the ground with my feet so that they wouldn't crush my body. I suddenly realized that I was on 26th of July Street. They pushed me onto a minibus with no license plates. Three of them held me and tried to push me inside the bus. I stood my ground, holding onto the door of the bus and refusing to get in. At a glance, I saw that the minibus was filled with unconscious young demonstrators. The three men began to feel me up as they continued to shove me into the bus. I was at once disgusted and disarmed, because I couldn't defend myself and my body. But I refused to go to the back of the bus.

"Get in—all the way in the back."

"No, I won't go to the back. I want to sit at the front by the window."

One of them pushed me forward, so I fell next to a young man who lay on the front seat. I sat up and pushed him away a little so I could be near the window. I suddenly remembered how we had liberated the demonstrators who had been arrested on the bus in Shubra. I tried to maneuver the window, but it was very heavy and difficult to break with my bare hands. I waved to passersby for help but no one moved. Suddenly, I spotted a friend by the door of the bus. I called out so that he would see me and know that I had been arrested, but he didn't respond; he just kept hanging onto the door of the bus without getting in. I saw him backing off. I tried to call a friend to let him know that I had been arrested but the line was busy. The driver saw me and reported me. They came and grabbed me from inside the bus. They started slapping me again.

"Who are you talking to, girl?"

They seized my cell phone and threw me out of the van and to the ground. I got up and straightened my clothes. I took a deep breath and got ready to swear at them. One of them pushed me.

"Get out of here this minute."

A young woman I did not know held onto me and moved me away.

I walked toward Merit, not quite knowing which street I was on. On the way, I met some friends who had been with me at the demonstration. We made sure that we were all well. They asked me, "Why didn't you run when you saw the riot police?"

"I did run, but then I saw that they had arrested a young man and were hitting and swearing at him. So I started to swear at them."

"That's why they beat you up. Because you can't keep your mouth shut."

"It's just not on. How can I be demonstrating for the rule of justice and dignity and then see someone get beaten and just shut up? I'd be a hypocrite."

I finally got to Merit and told those who were there what had happened. The owner of the publishing house advised me to file a complaint at the Hisham Mubarak Center for Human Rights. He gave me their numbers, but their lines were all busy. They were obviously inundated with complaints. I asked one of my friends to call his brother who worked for the center. He smiled but did not answer. I kept insisting and he kept nodding dismissively. I was upset but kept it to myself. I left Merit and went to Zahrat al-Bustan coffeehouse where I talked with friends about the events of the day. Suddenly, a gigantic man in a black coat appeared. He stopped to inspect the area: the coffeehouse itself, as well as the street and alleyway where customers were seated at tables. A general sense of unease hung over the place; people started to leave and the waiters began to remove the tables and chairs. I also felt uneasy about this mysterious man's presence.

"He must be with State Security."

"I'm going back to Merit."

"Would you like me to walk back with you?" one of my friends asked.

"I'll be okay; it's just around the corner."

I took a couple of steps and then stopped. I was a bit shaken so I signaled to my friend, "Yes, walk with me. I'm scared."

I rang my parents from Merit to let them know I was well and to tell them that my cell phone had been stolen. I had to make up answers for their questions, because I didn't want them to worry. Luckily, all the bruised areas were on my back and sides and it was winter. They wouldn't see the bruises. I hung up.

"Did you get the medication?"

"Yes, Mama."

Thank God I had left my handbag in Merit before going to the demonstration. Otherwise, the medication, my ID, and my camera would have been gone too.

We heard that there was another demonstration on Champollion Street. The owner of the publishing house and several other friends went to join. I stayed behind because my side was beginning to ache even more than when I was being beaten. Gradually, those who had left Merit came back one by one. After midnight, the friend who had ignored my request that he call his brother about my complaint also came back. We gathered around him. His glasses had been smashed, one of his eyes was completely swollen, and his entire face was full of bruises. We made room for him to rest. I reached out to feel my own glasses. Thank God I was able to save them. We were both shortsighted. Even though I was really concerned for him, I still gave him a reproachful glance, but I don't know if he saw it without his glasses.

"You didn't want to call your brother for me. But now you're going to call him for yourself."

I wrote a testimony of what had happened to me and posted it on Facebook. These people had to be exposed.

3
Suez

Throughout my life, I have hated Suez. Not quite all my life but since I started working at the Suez Canal University, in Suez. Initially, I thought that this move would be a civilized transition to a harbor city, rich in petroleum, by the sea, and home to the canal. Instead, I found an ugly and completely neglected town with unpaved streets and dilapidated buildings, except for Port Tawfik, the cosmopolitan end of town, reserved for the senior employees of the Suez Canal Administration. How could a city with so much going for it be so poor and so ugly? Even though the majority of its population was a conservative immigrant community from Upper Egypt, most of its youth could be described as a bunch of unruly thugs. They were mostly unemployed, or in temporary jobs, and many of them were on drugs. Those who had more key jobs were not from Suez itself. Because of regular harassment, insults, and calls for women to wear the veil, I came to hate this city and to limit my interaction with it to the space of the university; a space that made me hate it even more. I never felt that I was in an academic context but rather a commercial, competitive atmosphere that was fraught with gossip, spitefulness, and hypocrisy that wasn't remotely related to knowledge. Even though under normal circumstances, thuggery was not at all acceptable, it had become, in the wake of the January 25 uprising, a synonym for popular pluck and had been upgraded to heroism. At the end of the day, these people were the grandchildren of the national heroes of the 1956 and 1973 wars, who had for one hundred days endured the siege and complete isolation of their city.

Thousands took to the streets in a peaceful march after Friday noon prayer from Midan al-Arbein to al-Gharib area and then to the administrative building of the governorate. Men, women, and young people from all classes. They held banners with the same slogans as those in Cairo and other cities:

"No to Another Term. No to Inheritance of Power."

"Constitutional Amendments."

"Dissolve the Fraudulent Parliament."

"No to Torture."

The chanting grew louder in front of the governorate building:

"State Security, State Security! Where's the state and where's the security?"

"Hosni Bey, Hosni Bey! Lentils cost ten pounds today!"

"Egypt, dearest, you've been wasted!"

"Damn you! Live with honor!"

Then they sang the famous simsimiya song: "Homes of Suez." The protestors returned to Midan al-Arbein for the afternoon prayer and continued to chant. The police officers began to tease them with insults and threats of arrest and detention. The protesters responded:

"Silmiya! Silmiya!"

But just as the police officers and State Security had run out of patience in Shubra, so too did they run out of patience in Suez. Upon the orders of the officers, the riot police conscripts started beating the demonstrators with sticks. State Security thugs made their way into the demonstration and abducted many men, young and old, to which the demonstrators chanted: "Let him go! Let him go!"

This was followed by teargas canisters, rubber bullets, and live ammunition. People dispersed and then regrouped around the families of those who had been arrested. They decided to stage a sit-in in front of al-Arbein Police Station to demand the release of those who had been detained. More chanting:

"Ya Gamal, tell your dad, the people of Suez hate you bad!"

"Tell al-Adli and his boss, the people will cut your hand off!"

The officers shot at the demonstrators from the rooftop of the police station. Men, young and old, dropped to the ground.

"The man is dead! Why are you doing this? Why?"

"Have mercy! Why are you shooting us?"

"The man is dead. Enough! Oh God, help us."

On the other side of the street, another man fell, bleeding heavily.

"Help him, help him."

"Get him to sit up, guys. Help him sit up."

"Is he still breathing?"

"Help him recite the Shahada."

"Say: *la ilaha illa allah*. Come on, say: *la ilaha illa allah*."

But the man had died before he could say anything. In reaction, the demonstrators threw stones and rocks at the riot police trucks.

The next day, the relatives of the martyrs of the day before gathered in front of the morgue to take the body of the first martyr. The gate to the morgue was locked and it seemed that the authorities were refusing to deliver the body to the family. The demonstrators were angry and denounced the Mubarak regime:

"A word of honesty, a word of truth! We say no, Mubarak, we say no to you!"

They chanted for the martyrs:

"Martyr, martyr, rest in peace! For our struggle will not cease!"

"A man born of a man, your blood will free every man!"

The riot police retaliated with teargas, water hoses, and live ammunition. The demonstrators dispersed and regrouped and started throwing stones at the riot police. They chased each other back and forth; the demonstrators set fire to old tires to obstruct the police and created roadblocks using garbage bins and metal traffic blocks. These were street battles. The armored police vehicles shot more bullets at the demonstrators as they chased them and ran them over.

Why this madness? Why? Isn't it the police who started it?

As a riposte, the demonstrators set al-Arbein Police Station on fire after liberating those who had been arrested. More chanting:

"Men, men of Suez! Men, men of Suez!"

A car dealer, reputed to be a drug dealer, shielded the police officers and secured their access to the rooftop of his shop, so they could shoot the demonstrators who, in turn, destroyed the new cars in the shop and turned over some police vehicles. The skirmishes continued until dawn, resulting in many casualties.

Thursday, January 27, 2011, Morning

Security forces called for reinforcements for Suez from Ismailiya, and the people of Suez called their relatives and friends in Ismailiya, inciting them to demonstrate so these reinforcements would have to be sent back. And people really did rise in protest and solidarity in Ismailiya, despite their reputation for being lethargic and generally not fond of Suez or its people, rightly considering their own city as the most important one in the Canal Zone.

According to *al-Ahram* newspaper, "Mubarak Monitors Recent Developments and Inquires after the Welfare of the Citizens in Suez." The situation got worse with the death of a fourth demonstrator. Moving and inspiring funerals for three martyrs were accompanied by ululations as the demonstrations and confrontations continued. The people demand the removal of the regime, and rightly so!

By noon, I called my department at the university. It was the last day of final exams and I was expected to be there that morning. News that the Desert Road to Suez had been blocked and the fact that I couldn't verify the situation on the ground prompted me to postpone my departure to Suez.

"What does the situation look like on your end?"

"It's just fine; business as usual. Why are you not on campus?"

"How can I be in this volatile situation?"

"Oh, it's just a couple of demonstrations in al-Arbein."

"What do you mean a couple of demonstrations? The whole country is on fire!"

"Yes, but we're working. This is none of our business."

I was demoralized. The uprising is in al-Arbein, not here. How long were people going to continue to be so passive? For how long would people only worry about getting things done on paper? In the afternoon, the head of the examination control administration called me at home.

"When will you come to grade the exams?"

"We have to wait and see what will happen tomorrow. Tomorrow is Friday."

"So what will happen? More demonstrations?"

"Yes, but tomorrow will be a big day. I will be joining and I don't know what will happen next."

"So when will you come to the university? We want to submit the grades."

"What grades are you talking about, sir? There is a revolution taking place in the country."

"The revolution is in Cairo, not here. So when are you coming?"

"I will come on Sunday, hopefully, inshaallah."

"No. You must come on Saturday."

"Okay, Saturday, but still, inshaallah."

But it was not God's will that I go. He willed something quite different.

The people of Suez persisted in their struggle against injustice without deliberately targeting the riot police conscripts, among whom there were many unintentional casualties. After all, they were helpless creatures.

When reinforcements arrived from Ismailiya, the people of Suez chanted "Silmiya! Silmiya!" and they refrained from attacking the Central Security conscripts.

"Don't attack them."

"Make way for them."

The demonstrators helped the conscripts out of their trucks as they clapped and chanted: "Our brothers, our brothers." The demonstrators attacked the officers and stripped them of their arms. The officers ran away. The demonstrators started setting the police trucks on fire, one after the other. Black smoke rose over the sky in al-Arbein and so did the voice of the people:

"Look! See! The people of Suez are out and free!"

The governor of Suez and the businessman—the car dealer—who was implicated in the deaths of the demonstrators fled. The charred al-Arbein Police Station was transformed into a museum. Young men stood in front of the gate inviting people to come inside: "The Museum of al-Arbein, formerly the police station; free entrance." Families flocked to the museum with their children. Suez had become a free city, the first liberated city. Suez had been liberated before Cairenes could get to the heart of Midan al-Tahrir on Friday evening. The liberation of Suez fueled the Friday of Rage all over the country.

For the first time ever, I felt proud that I worked in Suez. Hats off to the valiant people of Suez!

4
Thursday, January 27, 2011

Morning.

Al-Ahram newspaper: Report on Events during the Past Two Days, 27 January 2011

Downtown Cairo witnessed a massive demonstration in the afternoon that started in front of the Lawyers' Syndicate and in which young lawyers and members of the April 6 and Kefaya movements participated.

The protesters chanted slogans against the state and demanded freedom of expression, democratic practices, and a halt to the rise in costs of living. They marched to Ramsis and 26th of July streets bringing traffic to a complete standstill. Security forces handled them, leading to skirmishes between the protestors and security, as well as injuries on both sides.

The early hours of the morning witnessed regrettable events in Tahrir Square and the surrounding area when some five thousand protestors started throwing stones at the security officers who were trying to break up the demonstrators, who had gathered in the midan for more than nine hours, having announced that they would remain there.

A security source stated that the protestors' decision to remain in Tahrir and their refusal to listen to pleas to abide by legal norms had led to an escalation of the situation. They had called on more protestors to join them and had bypassed acceptable codes of peaceful protest, engaging in acts of sabotage and attempts to paralyze life in the downtown area.

Since the early hours of the morning security forces used water hoses and tear gas to break up the demonstrations. But the protestors persisted in acts of sabotage, setting police vehicles on fire in Abdel Moneim Riyad Square. They also attempted to set a public structure, as well as private and public vehicles, on fire on the Nile Corniche.

The source reported that security forces had exercised extreme restraint throughout January 25, but that instigators of the protest succeeded in gathering hundreds of youth against the security forces. Contrary to propaganda on satellite channels, the security source denied that hundreds of thousands of Egyptians had taken to the streets and confirmed that the main demonstrations were restricted to the Tahrir area only and that the numbers were around ten thousand and had quickly decreased to some five thousand protestors. He added that the total participation of protestors in other governorates matched that number and had dispersed upon being warned.

The source stated that the Ministry of Interior called on citizens to reject attempts at exploiting their problems and to be aware of the consequences of inciting lay people in an attempt to generate chaos and misrepresent the current situation in the country. The source added that legal action had been taken against those arrested and that the office of the prosecutor would begin investigations into all cases. The source further declared that no disruptive actions, marches, or demonstrations would be allowed, warning that legal action would be taken immediately and participants would be investigated.

With regard to incurred losses during the previous day, the source declared that the number of injured among the security forces totaled 162 nationwide. The events also led to three deaths in Suez and a total of 118 injured in three other governorates. Events also led to damage in public and private structures, shops, and to several security vehicles.

Demonstrations had started during the afternoon on January 25 in the areas of Dawaran Shubra and around the Supreme Court and Saad Zaghloul Mausoleum. Security forces had allowed protestors to freely express their opinions without imposing any security blockades so they marched to Ramsis Street and in other side streets in Shubra and Sabtiya, until they reached Tahrir.

Groups of protestors in front of the Supreme Court joined other groups marching from Downtown and Talaat Harb Street to Tahrir. There were some three thousand demonstrators. When disruptive elements attempted to storm the Egyptian Museum in Tahrir and engage foreign visitors, security forces handled them with water hoses. The first clashes between the protestors and security forces ensued: the protestors threw rocks at security forces and seized a civil defense vehicle, after forcing its driver out.

Undercover Muslim Brotherhood
Shortly after these clashes, security forces reopened Tahrir Square and allowed the demonstrators to chant their demands after they reiterated the peaceful nature of the demonstration and stopped their fellow protestors from throwing stones at security forces. To the surprise of the protestors themselves, the number of demonstrators quickly increased to ten thousand. After several skirmishes between the protestors and security forces during which protestors threw stones and empty bottles at security and at the parliament building, the area witnessed clashes among groups of demonstrators. The style used by many participants in the demonstrations revealed that members of the banned Muslim Brotherhood were dispersed among the crowds, who totaled some seven thousand protestors, exploiting the democratic climate that allows for freedom of expression in order to achieve their political goals and take control of the situation. They chanted religious slogans. Suddenly, the voiced demands for the good of the people changed into ones against the regime. Members of the Muslim Brotherhood publicly revealed their affiliation and the situation became more volatile, after they attacked public buildings, shops, and cars.

Audacity of Action
During the January 25 demonstrations, security forces identified groups of protestors who were not chanting with the others and were only engaged in throwing stones at security forces. Protestors fled after security forces handled them with water hoses and tear gas. Only the stone-throwing groups remained, but they, too, eventually fled.

In a different scene from these demonstrations, groups of saboteurs caught the teargas canisters in midair and threw them back at security forces. One protestor got on top of one of the security vehicles and tried to seize the teargas cannon from the police officer, but the latter succeeded in keeping it under his control. Many of the protestors seemed to be influenced by foreign agendas; they insisted on provoking security forces, even as they showed restraint. They chanted strange slogans like: "you will be tried and thrown in jail;" and "we'll see what you will say to the CIA."

Some illegitimate political groups deliberately exploited the protests by occupying part of the Tahrir Square central garden and attaching a microphone to the traffic light. Members of these political groups took turns delivering speeches and instigated the protestors to stage a sit-in in Tahrir Square. They said that the Egyptian youth has repeatedly been accused of sexual harassment and that by staging a sit-in in Tahrir they could rebuff these accusations and show that they were able to protect the women in the square.

Evening, Merit Publishing House

It was a boisterous gathering, as usual, but even more animated than usual as it was filled with writers, artists, and intellectuals. We discussed the role that we should play during this moment. We agreed to issue a statement that would express our position as writers and artists for change. We declared our solidarity with the Egyptian people in their demand for change, freedom, and democracy, and we denounced the regime's use of violence against peaceful protesters. We reconfirmed our intention to continue to protest until the downfall of this dictatorial regime and its symbols. Even though I don't really like statements that merely declare a position, this time, most of us had actually been on the streets and had participated in the demonstrations during the past couple of days. So, the words matched the deeds. We concluded the statement with the most celebrated line of poetry at that historic moment:

"If someday the people will to live,

Then fate must an answer give."

The sheer act of writing and reading this line of poetry made me feel strong and convinced me that we would be able to resurrect the people of this country. Fate would undoubtedly respond. When I say "we" I do not refer only to the intellectuals, but I mean all of us; we would all be resurrected and the spirit we had lost and that the regime sought to kill would return to us. We split into two groups: one composed the statement in Arabic and the other in English. We started collecting signatures. A Kuwaiti writer and friend who lived in Cairo arrived and joined in the enthusiasm and joy of what was taking place in Egypt. He told me that he had been trying to contact me since the day before, but that all he got was a recorded message saying that my phone was out of service. I laughed and told him about what had happened to me and that I had canceled my line in a desperate attempt to keep State Security from getting hold of my contact list. Immediately, and quite spontaneously, the Kuwaiti friend produced a cell phone and charger from his pocket and handed them to me.

"What's this? An iPhone? Oh, no!"

"Please accept it as a gift."

"No, I can't accept an iPhone! I wouldn't know how to use it!"

"Then learn."

"I don't want an iPhone. I want a Nokia, the one with a flashlight."

"Come on, take it and don't be ridiculous."

I took it, timidly. The group began to laugh and make fun of me.

"Lucky you! You got an iPhone!"

"I wish they had beaten me up and taken my phone during the demonstration."

"There's another guy who was beaten up and whose phone was taken during the demonstration."

"No, he got it back."

"How?"

"He was walking toward Tahrir and bumped into the Cairo chief security officer sitting at a table. He told him what had happened. So the officer said to him: "Go look on that table for your cell phone," pointing to a table nearby. The table was covered with cell phones. The guy went through the cell phones on the table and ended up finding his phone."

"I should have done that too, but I had no idea that there was a lost and found table for cell phones near KFC.

"Anyway, you just got yourself a better phone."

"Yes, the first accomplishment of the revolution!"

We tried to send the statement we had written to as many writers and artists as possible but no one could open their emails. We tried Facebook, but that didn't work either. We tried other web pages, but the Internet was not working and neither were our USB drives from any of the cell phone companies. We tried our phones but there was no network available.

"They did it! They cut us off from the world."

"Everyone already knows that there is a call for the Friday of Rage. Al Jazeera had also announced it before they started intercepting the channel."

"Now they're going to wipe us out and no one will see what they're doing. It will be a massacre."

A group of friends arrived with news that many protesters had been detained as they were coming out of the metro station heading toward the midan. Gloom hung over the place. Someone volunteered to tell the latest jokes.

"Okay, let's hear them."

"They've been saying that if Egypt persists, it will play Tunisia in the finals."

We laughed despite the anxiety.

"Give us another one."

"Apparently they've merged Mother's Day, Police Day, and Christmas into one day and have called it Mother-Fucking Police Day."

"That's a good one!"

"More!"

Rocking between laughter and anxiety, we decided to leave and meet up the next morning at Merit to join the demonstrations after Friday prayer.

5
January 28, 2011,
Friday of Rage

1

I woke up early, feeling motivated, hopeful, and optimistic even though I had not slept enough and despite all the warnings against demonstrations issued by the Ministry of Interior and tirelessly broadcast on television—not to mention the worry and fear in my parents' eyes. I read the directives for the demonstrations that I had saved on my computer and that had been posted on several pages before the Internet had been cut off on Thursday night:

> The demonstrations will be peaceful. We are peaceful and are not calling for violence. We must exercise self-restraint and must not do anything against the law, subject people's lives to danger, or tamper with any public or private property. Please bring an Egyptian flag but not any other banner or sign that designates a political party or group or organization or sectarian affiliation. Today is a day for all Egyptians, because we are calling for equal rights and social justice. We do not want divisions. The riot police conscript is part of the draft; he works twenty hours a day; his misfortune is that he is part of the draft at this particular moment. Most of these conscripts do not want to beat people up. Protect yourself but do not endanger the lives of these conscripts.

Then, I read all the advice that many Tunisian friends had sent after the call for the Friday of Rage:

Important: please circulate widely. From Tunisia, the sister nation, to all our revolutionary brothers and sisters in Egypt:

1) Use black spray or paint to cover the windshields of the armored vehicles to paralyze their movement.

2) Wear plastic bags to protect yourselves from electrical shocks and protect your legs with anti-shock tape, this has worked for us in Tunisia.

3) Important: Rinse your face with Coca-Cola. It immediately counters the effect of teargas; we have tried this in Tunisia and it has rendered their canisters ineffective. God be with you, Egyptians!

4) How to incapacitate armored vehicles and security trucks: Shove a piece of cloth into the exhaust pipe to block the exhaust; better still, use a piece of wood wrapped in wet cloth. You can also use the sleeve of a shirt. This will block the engine for about seven seconds, and it will bring the car and water hose to a halt. Note that if you remove the cloth, the vehicle will run again. This idea was used on Israeli tanks during the 1973 war and was exceedingly effective.

I smiled as I read the instructions, even though it felt like I was going to war. I wore comfortable clothes and grabbed a coat and scarf. My parents stood in the hallway, following my movements. I went to the kitchen and took a bottle of vinegar, a bottle of water, and some onions. I looked for the Egyptian flag I had bought the year before to cheer on the Egyptian soccer team when it won the African Cup. I couldn't find it. I put everything in my backpack and prepared to leave. My father and mother moved toward me, eyeing me as if I were off to a war zone.

"You still insist on going?"

"Everybody is going, Mama."

"They are all young men and boys, not girls."

"Girls and women have been there from the first day."

"We have invested in you and your education until you have become a professor. I want you to be of benefit to the country, not get yourself killed."

"Baba, do you really believe that all the people going are just good-for-nothings?"

"I'm just worried about you. You are in a country that has no respect for human beings or for the law."

"That's precisely why we're all going: to change the regime."

He threw his arms up in the air.

"What can I say? Go. God be with you and protect you all. Take good care of yourself."

"Don't worry, Baba. Whatever will be, will be!"

They each gave me a long hug and kissed me. My father pressed my hand and then let go of it.

"Please call us whenever you can."

"I will."

2

Should I go to Merit through Tahrir or through Downtown? No need to take risks. I might get arrested in Tahrir like many others. I took the bus to Midan Abdel Moneim Riyad. The streets were relatively empty and quiet. There were only the riot police trucks and the armored vehicles surrounding most of the streets in Downtown starting from Midan Ramsis and probably other major squares. I walked across the midan to Mahmoud Bassiouni Street. I saw a convoy of riot police conscripts at the corner taking orders from their officers: "The most important thing is to protect your face. You must always have your shield and stick in hand. They are many, but with God's help, we can still defeat them even if we are less in number: *How many a small company has overcome a large company by permission of Allah. And Allah is with the patient.*"

Holy shit! So we're unbelievers! I think that was the verse revealed to the Prophet during the Battle of Uhud. I looked at the conscripts: they seemed miserable. It was probably the first time the officers had addressed them in this manner. And for the first time ever, we were the majority and they were the minority. Despite the horrific religious insinuation that we were unbelievers, I held my tongue and did not comment on what the officers were saying. I walked to Qasr al-Nil Street, heading toward Merit. The place was not open yet. Another friend arrived. We both stood at the entrance to the building for a couple of minutes, then we decided to go to After Eight and wait there. We ordered tea and coffee and started to chat.

"Did you hear the latest joke? My son was telling it this morning."

"Tell me."

"They say they've canceled Friday from the week and we'll go straight to Saturday."

"Cowardice reigns. The government's, I mean."

"There's also a new fatwa that permits skipping Friday prayer in case of public danger."

"No way!"

"I swear to God! My son's friends called him up this morning and told him so."

"Anything is possible in this country. The mufti is their man, after-all."

"But still, people will come in the thousands after Friday prayer. They won't listen to fatwas and stuff like that. Egyptians have woken up."

We noticed that there was a group of men sitting beside us who were eavesdropping on our conversation. The watchfulness that marked their features was different from that that marked ours.

"Who are they? Detectives?"

"They look like they might be State Security."

We could hear helicopters hovering quite low in the Downtown sky and we could actually see them through the open passageway near After Eight.

"I saw another helicopter on my way here from Giza. I thought it was because ElBaradei was going to Friday prayer in the neighborhood."

"That is pretty concerning."

"Lower your voice. These detectives hear everything."

"Let's go. I don't feel safe around here. Merit should be open by now."

We got up, leaving our unfinished tea and coffee behind. We paid the bill and left.

3

Merit Publishing House

Many friends and other people I didn't know began to arrive. We could overhear parts of the Friday sermon in some mosque, probably on Huda Shaarawi Street, blasting from an amplifier that carried the imam's shrieking voice. It seemed like a very long sermon. We could make out words like "obedience," "guardian," "the prohibition of demonstrations in Islamic law." Then we heard a lot of noise and commotion followed by "Allahu Akbar!" It sounded like one of the people present in the mosque had interrupted the imam and asked him to begin noon prayer. It seemed like people were fed up and wanted to get out of the mosque. One of our friends came in giggling.

"What are you laughing at?" we all asked in the same breath.

He pulled himself together and began telling us about what he had seen and heard at the corner of Qasr al-Nil Street. The police officers were patting the conscripts on their shoulders, urging them to be composed. They were still repeating the same Qur'anic verse, *How many a small company has overcome a large company by permission of Allah. And Allah is with the patient.* We all cracked up laughing. Others told similar stories and we were all ecstatic that we were "the large company" for a change.

The imam ended the noon prayer with its formulaic closure: *al-salamu alaykum wa rahmatu llah.*

The imam had barely started the second "*al-salam . . .*" when we overheard:

"Long live Egypt! Long live Egypt!"

"The people demand the removal of the regime!"

It seemed that the demonstration had erupted somewhere near Midan Talaat Harb. It took one person inside the mosque chanting, "Long live Egypt" for all the others to follow suit: "Long live Egypt!"

We rushed to the windows; even though we couldn't see anything, we could hear thundering voices. The teargas was very thick, so we quickly shut the windows, but the gas still leaked into the apartment. We were smothered by the smell and started coughing continuously, beginning to feel faint. Tears and burning nostrils, when most of us already suffered from allergies. I suddenly remembered the vinegar and reached for the bottle in my bag. I started pouring some on the tips of people's scarves and shawls to cover our nostrils.

"Damn them! They're blinding us."

We remained in our places until the effect of the gas had subsided. One of the women wanted to go out and see what was happening.

"No one is to go out alone."

Two other friends decided to go with her. All three left. A gas canister was thrown right in front of them as they were making their way out of the building. They inhaled a huge quantity in one go. They tried to help each other back up to the first floor where the Merit office was located. The smoke filled the entrance and the stairway and made its way into people's apartments. How mean could they get, throwing gas canisters at apartment buildings and at people inside their homes?

"God help us!"

We hurried toward those who were choking on the gas to give them vinegar and onions. We poured Coca-Cola on their faces. I searched for the eyedrops I had bought the day before and had left in the Merit office just in case. I finally found them in one of the drawers and used them for those who had gone out into the street, and then for the rest of us.

"It looks like this will be a very bad day."

I opened the window and looked out onto the street. It was completely empty. Suddenly, a black-and-white cab and another white car arrived. They stopped in front of a row of policemen. There seemed to be a brief conversation between them. Perhaps the passengers were trying to get to Midan al-Tahrir. One of the officers was going through some papers. A group of men with sticks came out of the cars and stood near the officer. The cab driver backed up and headed toward Midan Talaat Harb. The white car headed toward the garage of Misr Insurance Company. The security at the garage refused to let the car through. The driver started yelling, "Don't you know who I am?"

He continued to grumble and swear, but the security guards stood their ground.

"It's against regulations, sir. This is a private garage."

"Good for them!"

The driver had to go and park in another public garage and then he joined the other plainclothes thugs with sticks. They were talking and laughing with the officers.

We had no option but to sit in front of the television screen to follow what was happening elsewhere on Al Jazeera. Hundreds of thousands had gone out to public squares all over Egypt in most of the governorates. Police stations and NDP offices were being burned down in several areas. The riot police were using water cannons against people praying in Alexandria and in other cities. They were attacking them with gas canisters as soon as they left the mosques in different places. Atrocious!

They started intercepting Al Jazeera. It finally stopped broadcasting. We flipped through the channels and watched some of the Egyptian channels out of curiosity. Nothing but silly films and even sillier songs! We no longer had cell phones or Internet or Al Jazeera. What were we going to stay indoors for? Let's go back to the street again. We couldn't get through to Tahrir because it was completely blocked. Midan Talaat Harb was infested with undercover agents and State Security in plain clothes, given away by their facial expressions.

We remained at the edge of the midan where we watched the demonstrators as they assembled from different side streets, chanting. The riot police forces started advancing from Qasr al-Nil and Mahmoud Bassiouni streets. Some of the thugs rushed forward and started attacking the demonstrators with sticks. They arrested some of them. The demonstrators continued to chant, "Silmiya! Silmiya!" There was another teargas attack. We ran in all directions. I placed the tip of my scarf across my nostrils and inhaled the vinegar. The street was flooded with bottles of water, vinegar, and onions that were thrown to the demonstrators by people from balconies and windows. The demonstrators were in the midst of the riot police conscripts who had started collapsing on the ground because of the amount of teargas they had inhaled. Everyone was using vinegar and onion and chanting, "The people demand the removal of the regime!" I passed on the tip of my scarf to some of the conscripts who were standing near me.

"I don't want any."

I placed it over their nostrils despite their protests.

"Inhale."

They looked at me curiously, at once annoyed, embarrassed, and uncomfortable.

"It's true that what you are doing is criminal, but you are human beings at the end of the day."

I didn't wait for their reaction and started walking briskly toward Merit through the passageway near After Eight. I had made a good decision, as the riot police forces had retreated halfway down the street so that they stood almost in front of the Merit apartment building. No sooner was I inside the building than they started firing a torrent of rubber bullets. We took pictures of them from the Merit office windows and it seemed that other people in the building were doing the same. The riot police officer, a rather flabby, bald man, began yelling at the residents of the building, "Get inside!"

He had seen us taking pictures, so he started insulting us in the vilest language.

"Let them take pictures, these sons of . . . ."

One of our friends got very angry and suggested that we throw empty bottles and boiling water at them.

"Nothing rash, please! No need to challenge them. They'll come and beat us up and arrest us. We're taking pictures of them and that's enough."

"Yes, let's not do that. They'll come up and destroy the office, and this is Hashem's office at the end of the day. We have to protect the space we're in."

We watched from behind the windowpane as the riot police advanced and retreated toward Midan Talaat Harb with the flow of the demonstrators. But they didn't move too far away from the building. We would not be able to get out. We went to the rooftop to watch what was happening on the street. The Cairo skyline was saturated with smoke and Midan al-Tahrir was completely empty. Where were all the demonstrators who were supposed to be arriving from all over Cairo? Were we going to remain besieged and not be able to make it to Tahrir? Please God, help us defeat them. We couldn't just turn back now; we had to continue.

We kept going up and down between the first floor and the rooftop. We could overhear chanting that rose and fell to the rhythm of the teargas and rubber bullets. We felt confined and paralyzed. The sun was about to set. We prayed to God for victory. It was the worst thing to be asking God to help you defeat other Egyptians. But what could we do?

4

Suddenly the street was filled with demonstrators. Allahu Akbar! The street was now open; the midan was open. We ran down to the street. The demonstrators were entering the midan. The riot police conscripts were taking off their uniforms and running. One of them asked me, crying, "Could you please tell me how to get to Ramsis Railway Station?"

"Don't be afraid. Keep walking straight and then make a left. Try to get there through Downtown."

We went into the midan. We were met with new waves of teargas. We retreated. Some of us fell to the ground. Those who fell were quickly carried off and given anti-gas treatment.

"Why are you retreating? Where's your manliness?" said one of the young demonstrators.

They stormed the midan once more.

I stood on the sidewalk to catch my breath. Thugs passed by in front of me. I opened my mouth to let people know, but my voice did not come out. One of them saw me and placed his finger on his mouth as a sign that I should be quiet. Everyone ran toward Tahrir. Only the officers and conscripts were running in the opposite direction. They had been stripped of their masks, their shields, their sticks, their rifles, and their helmets. I couldn't believe my eyes. The police was retreating, crestfallen and empty-handed, but not injured by the demonstrators. Thank you, God!

The Qasr al-Nil Bridge frontline was still blocked. Thousands were stranded on the bridge besieged by teargas that was being rained on them. The demonstrators picked up the canisters and threw them into the Nile. There were many deaths and injuries. The riot police opened the horrible water cannons on the demonstrators; an armored vehicle moved forward and tried to run over the demonstrators; the officers started firing bullets at the demonstrators in front of them. The demonstrators retreated as they chanted energetically:

"Shame on you, shame on you! An Egyptian brother shoots at you!"

I tried to put myself in their place: besieged and suffocating. I cried where I stood. One of the officers, overwhelmed by the scene, threw the gas canisters into the Nile; he took off his uniform and joined the demonstrators. They embraced him. One of the conscripts refused to fire, so the officer shot him. He fell to the ground and the officer continued to shoot at the demonstrators. A new wave of demonstrators from Imbaba, Giza, and Warraq came to the rescue. They were being led by fearless young men that I, and those like me from the middle class, would normally describe as 'rough' bordering on thugs. They moved forward dragging along with them the metal roadblocks, abandoned police kiosks, and car tires they had found on their way. They couldn't care less about the gas or the bullets. They confronted the conscripts and the officers with their bare chests, advancing through their barriers: "The people demand the removal of the regime," period. They opened up the midan to the demonstrators and merged with the thousands who were advancing from Downtown and Midan Abdel Moneim Riyad.

"Long live Egypt! Allahu Akbar!"

Egyptians are beautiful!

There was more teargas and we could hear shooting in the direction of Qasr al-Aini Street. I think they were trying to keep us away from the Ministry of Interior and from the Parliament. We regrouped at a safe distance from the shooting and shelling. The demonstrators continued to hurl the canisters back at those who initially threw them.

Suddenly, there was quiet: the teargas and bullets stopped. Two ambulances made their way into the midan. The demonstrators made way for them. A bit later, we heard heavy shooting coming from the direction of Qasr al-Aini Street. Another two ambulances arrived. The demonstrators stopped them and pounded on their doors. One of the demonstrators said, "Search these ambulances."

"Those sons of bitches are using even the ambulances!"

The demonstrators brought out the weapons and ammunition from the ambulances and let the drivers go through unharmed. They started distributing the loot randomly for it was dark in the midan. Some took bullets; others took rifles. A group of demonstrators decided to go to the office of Al Jazeera to show the weapons and have them report on what had happened. Others preferred to keep the loot as a souvenir from the battle. When I went back to Merit I found a display of several kinds of bullets (live and rubber), the shields of the riot police conscripts, their helmets, sticks, and canisters of long-expired teargas.

"The sons of bitches are attacking us with expired weapons!"

"They don't think we're worth new canisters. Shame on the Ministry of Interior! They're doing it on the cheap!"

5
Breaking news
Curfew imposed in Cairo, Alexandria, and Suez from 4 p.m. to 2 a.m.

Hundreds of thousands fill the streets and the squares until after 6 p.m.

"They can shove their curfew."

"Or they can enforce it on themselves."

More breaking news: The army is deployed on the streets.

"What does that mean? Will the army attack us?"

"The army will never attack the people."

Breaking news again: The president will give a speech shortly.

"I wonder what he will say."

"Will he step down?"

"If he does, we will have outdone Tunisia!"

"Actually, we have already outdone them. Our army was deployed three days after the revolution. In Tunisia, the army only stepped in at the very end. Ours is the fastest revolution in history."

Some of our friends returned to Merit with news that the headquarters of the NDP was in flames. I went with a couple of friends to watch this historic moment. We couldn't get too close because of the crowds and we were not quite sure whether the fire started inside or outside the building. We were certain, however, that a group of men were throwing Molotov cocktails at the building while chanting,

"I swear by Egypt, its skies and its lands, this ruin is on NDP hands!"

The flames rose inside the building. Of course I don't like fires, but in this case, I was moved by a mixture of happiness and vengeance. There was a feeling of victory as I watched parts of the building collapse and as the flames devoured several floors. From where I stood, I could only see the flames and the black smoke rising in the sky over Midan Abdel Moneim Riyad after it had been saturated with the fumes from the teargas. Suddenly, we could see groups of men making their way through the crowds, dragging along armchairs, tables, living room furniture, side lamps, LCD screens. I cracked up laughing. "Unbelievable! What are they taking armchairs for?"

"They're grabbing whatever they can get their hands on out of spite."

"Yes, I know, but they're very heavy."

"Look over there. Right next door to the NDP is the National Council for Women."

"I can't see properly."

"Can't you see the guys carrying laptops out of there too?"

"Incredible!"

"This must be a gang. They're passing them on to each other. It's not just the armchairs, you see."

"If you steal, steal a laptop, not an armchair."

Before we started heading back to Merit, we heard people screaming and hundreds running in the direction of the Egyptian Museum. We joined them.

"The museum is burning, guys. We have to save it," said one of the men.

"It will be looted!"

Hundreds joined hands and arms to form rows of human chains to surround the museum and protect it. Thank God the flames from the NDP headquarters did not reach it. The demonstrators arrested some people in the garden of the museum who were trying to steal. They gave them a good beating.

"This is our civilization and history, you sons of bitches."

They body searched them and seized their papers.

"Holy shit! They're cops!"

"Of course, the guards themselves are the thieves."

We laughed as they continued to beat them. Then they tied them up.

"They deserve it!"

We went back to Merit after we were sure that the museum was safe. Many other friends arrived. Everyone looked exhausted and worn out, as if they had just returned from the battlefront. Disheveled clothes, faces smeared with dirt, sweat, and traces of blood. We gave our seats to the newcomers. Some collapsed on the sofa; others sprawled on the floor; some went to wash, while others started sharing stories of scenes from the demonstrations with great enthusiasm.

"I went to Friday prayer at the Mosque of Sayyida Aisha with some friends. The imam had barely finished the prayer when someone stood up and started chanting, 'The people demand the removal of the regime.' Just as we were about to leave the mosque, the riot police started shelling us with teargas and rubber bullets. We kept saying, 'Silmiya, silmiya,' but they just went on with the shelling. We tried to find a place to hide as the gas and rubber bullets continued to rain on people's homes. Suddenly, the people of the neighborhood came out chanting 'Mubarak, you motherfucker! Dirty government, you sons of bitches! Illegitimate, you sons of bitches!' They all had hatchets and pocketknives and they stabbed every officer and policeman they could get their hands on. The women dangled baskets from their balconies and windows. We thought they were sending us vinegar and onions, but they were actually sending bottles full of gasoline and the guys started making Molotov cocktails and throwing them at the armored vehicles and conscripts. In two or three hours, the vehicles had been burned out and the police had run away and the police station had been totally burned down."

"Incredible."

"Did they really think that people would take this quietly?"

"We are the people, at the end of the day. But the guys from these informal neighborhoods are quite something. We wouldn't know how to do what they've done. We're definitely not a match for them."

"After we finished praying today, some young guys from our neighborhood started a demonstration and were chanting, 'Illegitimate, illegitimate! Hosni Mubarak is illegitimate!' So I joined them. The riot police and their thugs attacked us and beat us up. They abducted a couple of protestors, I think, and then they started with the teargas. Then the officers began shooting at us, so we started running and the demonstrators were separated. After a while, we regrouped when we saw the brave guys from Talbiya heading confidently toward us. I told myself that they would make this day and lead us forward. And they did! They were taking drugs, jumping on the armored vehicles and then grabbed a policeman inside it and pulled him out. They kept this up with the police, despite the gas and the bullets. They went back and forth until the police withdrew to their base area. In seconds, they surrounded them and the guys who had gone up to the rooftops showered them with stones and Molotov cocktails. Within an hour, the riot police conscripts had run away and the officers took off their uniforms and ran too."

"These are the same guys who get screwed in the police stations. They know how to deal with the cops."

"Guys, this story must be recorded."

One of our friends walked in looking for her husband.

"Don't worry. He's here, in the bathroom."

"Thank God! I was so worried about him."

"Where were you?"

"I was at home with the kids and my friends' kids as well. We drew lots on who would babysit and I got stuck at home and they all left. I spent the evening between the living room and the balcony. We were swamped with teargas. The sky in Dokki and Agouza was all white; you couldn't see a thing. And the kids were all coughing and I just didn't know what to do. I sat on the balcony crying and praying to God. I was worried about those who had left and was wondering who would return and who would not. I wanted to join them and be with them. When the shooting stopped my mom came over and I was able to leave."

I suddenly remembered my parents. They must be very worried about me. I called them from the office phone and let them know that I was well. They were both happy to hear my voice.

"The army is on the street, guys," yelled one of the people who had been watching television. We all gathered around the screen to watch the army vehicles filing onto the Corniche, heading toward the TV Building in Maspero. One of the vehicles stalled, so the protestors pushed it forward. The officers were greeting the protestors and were holding red flags.

"Ha! What a start! An old armored vehicle that stalls before it even gets there!"

"What's really great is that the protestors are pushing it!"

"Pity that the image is shot from a distance! I would have liked to see the expression on the faces of the army officers."

Breaking news: Mubarak will address the nation shortly.

"We've been waiting for the past three hours. When is he going to speak?"

"Shame on him! Can't keep his word."

"Doesn't he know that we have other things to do? He thinks the people have nothing better to do."

We waited for the president's speech.

The wait was long. So we continued to watch the arrival of the army vehicles and tanks in Tahrir.

6

The Army

My relationship with the army is encapsulated in my Niva car. It is a Russian-made Lada that the army uses in the desert. Even though I had often seen it stranded on the road, the fact that the army was using it, encouraged me to buy it. Often army personnel on the Cairo–Suez road stop me to give them a ride. As soon as they realize that the driver is a woman they smile and raise their hands apologetically. The headquarters of the Third Army and the memorial for its martyrs are on the way to Suez, where I work. I always salute the martyrs as I drive past the memorial as a tribute to our soldiers who died during the October 1973 War with Israel. The only time I had to deal with the army was at the checkpoint at the Ahmed Hamdi Tunnel on the way back from southern Sinai in an East Delta bus. The bus stopped and we all got out, so they could search our luggage for weapons and drugs. The army conscripts brought in a famished dog, most probably a stray, to sniff our bags. The minute he came near me he started barking nonstop. I almost died! Everyone was watching me and I was looking around me. One of the officers politely asked if he could search my bags.

"Go ahead."

I gave him the bag as if getting rid of incriminating proof, while the crazy dog continued to bark. The officer brought out a plastic bag and opened it. There was a half-eaten kofta sandwich in the bag that I had forgotten all about. The officer and the passengers all started laughing.

"Have pity on your dog and feed him properly. He scared the Hell out of me!"

"We apologize," said the officer politely, while still laughing. He gave me back the sandwich.

"No, I don't want it. Give it to the dog."

This is how I like the army: from a distance. I like their politeness and good nature. I like their discipline and may even like their uniform.

But the army was being deployed on the streets on orders from the president of the republic, as he is commander-in-chief of the Armed Forces. What will the army do to us? Will it like us, as we like it? Will it side with us or against us? Will it finish us off, after the police failed? The same thoughts were in the minds and words of the protestors. We were all somewhat anxious. No one could tell for sure whether the army was with us or against us. Army jeeps began to roll in; these were probably Presidential Guard jeeps. The demonstrators rushed forward and surrounded them. The soldiers inside smiled mysteriously, but the demonstrators remained divided: Some tried to attack the jeeps, while others were trying to protect the army; some were asking the officers and the soldiers to stay near the museum that the demonstrators had surrounded in the thousands to protect. The cars tried to make their way through. The incident with the ambulances that had been transporting weapons was still fresh in people's minds. Finally, the demonstrators got the soldiers out of their army jeeps, which they searched with small flashlights. The demonstrators found weapons and teargas. They immediately started setting the jeeps on fire. A Presidential Guard armored vehicle arrived on the scene and tried to make its way through to the Ministry of Interior. The demonstrators stopped it and searched it. The soldiers ran toward the museum. The demonstrators seized the bullets, as if they were loot from battle, and then they set the armored vehicle on fire.

"What exactly is this 'Presidential Guard'?"

"It is part of the army, but it takes its orders from the president and is loyal to him."

"So they might attack us."

"Possibly, no one knows for sure what might happen. God be with us."

A long line of army tanks began to arrive, coming from the direction of Midan Abdel Moneim Riyad. The demonstrators jumped up on the tanks and sat on them. They held the hands of the soldiers and officers and chanted: "The army and the people are one hand." The officers and soldiers, who seemed overwhelmed and somewhat taken aback, had no choice but to chant along to reassure the protestors.

"Don't worry. We are on your side."

Perhaps that was the case. But perhaps the thousands that besieged them and the burned-out army jeeps and armored vehicle made them realize that they couldn't attack the people, for they would not allow that and were capable of fighting back. But we didn't want a confrontation with the army. We wanted them to be with us.

The tanks surrounded all the entrance points to the midan. The protestors gathered around them and spray-painted slogans like "Down with, down with Hosni Mubarak."

"There go your tanks, Hosni Mubarak!"

I held on to a friend's arm so that we would not lose each other in the crowds as we watched the arrival of more tanks. He asked me to take his photo with my cell-phone camera.

"Are you serious? You want your picture taken in front of a tank?" I asked him, laughing.

"Yes, what's the big deal?"

"You're acting like a child!"

"Everybody is having their picture taken next to the tanks and on top of the tanks and with the soldiers."

I grabbed my cell phone and took several pictures of him.

"Now it's your turn. Let me take your picture."

"No!" I replied, laughing.

But then I went and stood in front of a tank and raised my arm with the victory sign, while still giggling. He took several pictures.

The presence of the tanks in the midan was actually quite exciting. I'd never seen a tank on the street before, at least not tanks with slogans saying "Down with Hosni Mubarak" on them.

"Let's go chat with the soldiers and officers."

We circled around a tank and an armored vehicle and yelled as loud as we could, in our worn-out voices:

"Guys, we're your brothers and sisters. Please don't attack us. We're family, don't shoot at us. We're Egyptians too. We're all Egyptian."

We got almost the same answer from them all: "Don't worry."

We continued to tour the midan. I saw a soldier, or an officer perhaps (I couldn't quite make out his rank), standing on top of a tank trying to reassure people. I didn't know how to address him: soldier, officer?

"Captain, captain," I said.

"Yes," he answered, turning toward me.

"What is your rank, sir?"

"Lieutenant."

"What's your name?"

"Mohamed."

"Lieutenant Mohamed, sir."

"Yes?"

"May I make a pass at you? You're really cute!"

Everyone cracked up laughing: the officers, the soldiers, the protestors, and my friend and I as well. Lieutenant Mohamed smiled timidly. He tipped his army cap in salute. Obviously, I had no real intention of flirting with him, especially as I could barely make out his features in the dark that enveloped the midan, but I wanted to break the ice with the army and this was the first idea that came into my head. We passed cigarettes around to the soldiers but they refused to take them, despite the obvious craving written all over their faces. They were probably obeying orders not to take anything from the protestors. We resumed our tour of Tahrir, through the thousands of protestors until we reached Midan Abdel Moneim Riyad. Suddenly, people started scurrying and we heard the sound of shots. Someone yelled, "Run! They're shooting!" My friend dragged me and we ran to the building across from the museum where his clinic was. We stood inside the side entrance to the building. Suddenly, young protestors and children rushed toward us.

"They're shooting!"

"Who's shooting?"

"We don't know."

We went to the top floor of the building and into my friend's clinic, but it offered a very narrow view of the midan. We couldn't see a thing. We asked permission from the hotel owner on the same floor if we could take a look from his balcony. He let us in but we couldn't make out anything. The midan was quite dark and we could only hear the chants and the noise. We went back to the clinic, made tea, and sat down to rest for a while. We suddenly remembered the president's speech.

"Oh yeah, the president is supposed to give a speech."

My friend turned on the TV. The president was already on air.

"Finally!"

7

Mubarak's First Speech

Fellow citizens, I speak to you in very difficult times that dictate serious reflection from us all for the sake of our homeland.

"Oh, come on! Don't beat about the bush. Just say it!"

I have ordered the government to implement my instructions. This was apparent in the way the police force dealt with our youth and how they took the initiative to protect them at the beginning of the demonstrations out of respect for their right to peaceful protest.

"Of course! Couldn't ask for better protection, you liar, son of a liar!"

As president of the republic and based on the powers accorded me by the constitution, I have insisted time and again and will continue to insist that the people are the source of sovereignty, and I assert . . . .

"I will continue . . . . I will assert . . . . Damn it! He thinks he will still continue and assert?"

"Would make a nice ring tone: I will continue, continue, continue."

There is a fine line between freedom and chaos. Just as I side completely with the citizen's right to freedom of opinion, I uphold, with the same measure, the security and stability of Egypt.

"I side completely . . . . Who's the half-wit who wrote the speech? What does this mean? Who is threatening who with chaos?"

"Stability, again!"

This is a nation of institutions governed by a constitution and by the force of the law.

"Of course! The constitution you tailored to fit you and your sons."

"Guys, calm down a little. Let's hear him out."

We must take heed of the numerous examples that surround us and that have submerged the people in a chaotic setback. No democracy has been gained and no stability has been safeguarded.

"Stability!"

"I feel like I want to puke."

"I guess he's talking about Tunisia. He must feel sorry for Ben Ali."

I am aware of the people's legitimate aspirations, and I know their concerns and their suffering. I have never isolated myself from them. I work daily for their sake.

"He says 'I am aware.' Hope to God he says, 'Now I understand you,' like Ben Ali."

But they were quickly exploited by those who sought to spread chaos and to loot and to burn down public and private property, and destroy what we have built.

"'Exploited!' Aren't you ashamed of yourself?"

"Yeah we must be the fifth columnists who want total destruction."

"And what is it you built, you loser?"

"The metro and the Ring Road?"

"As they say, these are the accomplishments of the minister of transportation or the governor, not the accomplishments of the president of a nation."

"Be quiet, guys. Let's listen."

"He's not saying anything important. We've had it with rhetoric! We got enough of that at school."

My conviction is steadfast and unwavering.

"Unwavering! Wavering more like!"

Today, I address you not just as president of the republic, but as an Egyptian whose fate it was to shoulder the responsibility for this homeland—someone who has spent his entire life striving for its sake, in war and peace.

"What a dreadful fate indeed!"

"You are not the only one to have shouldered responsibility. My father is about your age, and he has worked his entire life and has served the country diligently."

The events of today and the past few days have cast fear in the hearts of the majority of the people for the welfare of Egypt and its future—people who are concerned that we will be dragged into more violence, chaos, destruction, and devastation. Today, I shoulder my primary responsibility to safeguard the security of the nation and its citizens. I will not allow this to happen. I will not allow . . . .

"What's this talk about 'I will not allow,' 'I will not allow'? Shut up, man!"

I have asked the government to submit its resignation, and tomorrow, I will take the initiative of forming a new government with new priorities and duties that respond to the demands of the current situation.

"'I have asked,' what a joke! We'll see, loser."

"The thing is, we don't want you, Mubarak."

"It's a bit too late now. Had he said all this on the night of January 25, it may have worked, we may have gone home. But now, it just can't work. The people want the removal of the entire regime, with Mubarak at its head."

We all went out into the street again. People were still chanting, "Down with, down with Hosni Mubarak!"

Once in a while, we would also hear, "The army and the people are one hand!"

The young protesters marched on and my friend and I walked back to Merit, through the thousands of people.

8

Merit Publishing House after Midnight

The place was packed. Some were following the commentary on the president's speech on TV, some were making fun of what he said, and some were in the back room listening to a young man's account of the demonstration in Ramsis, from which he had just come back with a riot police shield. Mohamed Hashem, the owner of Merit, said:

"Guys, we have to get food for the people in the midan."

A young group of friends volunteered to go with him to Abdeen. I sat on the floor and listened to the story that was being told:

"As soon as we got to Midan Ramsis, they started attacking us, even before we came near the police. Some retreated, while others dispersed into the side streets. This back and forth and stone throwing continued until late afternoon. We couldn't get beyond the first roadblock because of the violence. We stood at a distance of one hundred meters and decided to pray together. As we were praying, a new wave of demonstrators arrived; I think they may have come from Abbasiya or from Hadayeq al-Qubba. Anyway, the police started throwing teargas, hysterically. Some of the canisters landed where we were praying, but we continued to pray. Suddenly, people started chanting 'Allahu Akbar' and attacked the first police roadblock. A police car tried to make its way out, but the demonstrators set it on fire and beat up the officers and policemen who were all completely dazed. To tell you the truth, I felt sorry for them, but then, what they had done to us was also pretty brutal. I took this shield from one of the policemen and we ran back to Midan Ramsis. We found that some people had been stuck inside al-Fath Mosque and were being attacked with teargas. A bit later, the demonstrators made it to Midan Ramsis and the police retreated. The people who were inside the mosque quickly came out. They were all coughing; some passed out. One of the funny things was that there were two little boys: one around ten, the other about seven or eight. As soon as the teargas attack started, the ten-year-old told his brother, 'Get out of here now. Stay away from politics.' So the other said, 'No, I'm staying with you.' We cracked up laughing, despite the shooting. Then the demonstrators from Shubra and from Madinat Nasr arrived, so we all marched toward Galaa Street. The police attacked us viciously, so we ran to Aboul Ela Street, and people there threw us vinegar and onions from their balconies. Even the old man we bought Coca-Cola from refused to take money and the poor guy's entire kiosk went up in flames when a gas canister landed on it. But despite this horror, the most beautiful scene I saw was when a bearded young man ran toward the kiosk with a blanket in hand and was joined by another who was wearing a cross on a gold chain. The second guy clutched his arms together to help the bearded one climb up so he could put out the fire in the midst of continuing teargas attacks. I was really moved by that scene and I said to myself, 'May God protect Egypt and all Egyptians.' We kept scurrying back and forth until we forced the police to retreat. Suddenly, the officers started running and the policemen followed behind them. People set a couple of police cars on fire and the rest of the police turned around and ran. I never thought I'd see this in my life. The police were running away from us! Then we went to Tahrir and we found more police cars in front of the museum, trying to escape. Many people were coming to Tahrir from Downtown and everyone was chanting 'Allahu Akbar.'"

"Absolutely! Allahu Akbar!"

"But many people have died and have been injured. I saw several of them fall, covered in blood. But there was nothing that we could do to help them because there was so much shooting. All we could do was drag their bodies to the side and then God knows what happened to them. Have mercy on them, God, and all those who were injured."

After a while, Mohamed Hashem and the group that had left with him arrived with bags full of bread and groceries. We started making sandwiches: white cheese, roumi cheese, and halawa tahiniya. My arms were numb from opening the bread and spreading the cheese and the halawa. But we made three hundred sandwiches.

9

I took the supplies and went out with Hashem's daughters and two other friends to distribute them in the midan. The demonstrators had set up a citizens' checkpoint at the entrance of the building and the neighboring one to patrol the street. Exactly like Tunisia! We insisted that they take some sandwiches, but they adamantly refused.

"We live here," they said. "Give them to the people in the midan."

We headed toward the midan from Qasr al-Nil Street. It was relatively quiet. Some people were lying on the ground, others were exchanging stories, and some were strolling about. We walked toward the stone plinth in the midst of the midan, distributing the sandwiches along the way.

"Thank you so much."

One of the protestors opened a sandwich and then closed it up again and said, "Do you have white cheese? I don't like roumi cheese."

"Don't be picky!"

"Could I have a halawa sandwich, please?"

I exchanged the sandwiches and said, smiling, "Here you go, but don't harass us when the revolution is over."

"I swear it's not us! We don't do that kind of thing."

We laughed together and moved on to another group.

"Can I have another sandwich?"

"Sorry. Each person gets one, so we can give to as many people as possible."

"Okay, thanks."

I jokingly repeated the same request to them:

"Don't harass us after the revolution is over."

"I swear to God, it's not us. We don't do that kind of thing."

"No kidding? You all say that. So who is it that hassles us on the street then?"

We laughed and walked away. We ran into a group of bearded young men. I told my friends, "Let's go for these guys and try to win them over."

We stood in front of them, blocking their way.

"Have some, guys. The night is long and all the stores are closed."

Two of them timidly reached out to take the sandwiches. We smiled at them but didn't joke around. It was important that they know there are other people who look different but who are just as giving.

We had distributed all the sandwiches before getting to the central garden of the midan. We decided to go back to make some more. Before I had turned around, I spotted my sister at a distance distributing sandwiches like us.

"Maha!"

She turned around. I ran toward her and we hugged each other tight with joy, amazement, and pride. We both had tears in our eyes. I realized that I was not the only person to embrace her sister. Plenty of brothers and sisters and relatives were bumping into each other in the midan. I think that from each family there must have been one or two members, and many had not told their parents or relatives that they were going to the demonstrations. They all found each other in the midan.

"You came! How did you get here?"

"I came from Rehab with many others."

"No way! Residents of the Rehab compound also came?" I laughed out loud in disbelief.

"And why did you come?"

"I was actually quite hesitant. I wanted to come but I was afraid I'd get into trouble or be arrested and would not be able to finish my master's thesis. And, to tell you the truth, I just didn't believe that something would really happen. But then I felt ashamed that I was going to stay home to finish my thesis when people were out in the streets for Egypt."

"I'm very proud of you, Maha!"

"I'm happy too. I'm happy that I came. I can't believe what's happening. I'm happy that I got over my fear. I was very scared. I was even too scared to chant along, 'Down with, down with Hosni Mubarak.' Fear is such a terrible feeling. I don't want to inhale teargas anymore. I was going to die: I passed out and fell to the ground twice."

I held her very close and then released my grip for I know how fragile her body is and did not want to begin to imagine how she may have fainted and fallen.

"So tell me, how did you get here?"

"I took the Rehab bus and found people I knew from the American University in Cairo who were going to the demonstrations. Some went to Maadi and others wanted to go to al-Azhar. So we decided to go and pray at al-Azhar Mosque and then walk from there. After we finished praying, we found a group of demonstrators marching on al-Hussein Street. They were chanting along the way, 'Down with, down with Hosni Mubarak.' At the beginning, I was afraid to chant with them but they were chanting with such force, faith, and determination that I was very moved and tears came to my eyes. Then I found myself chanting aloud with them: 'Down with, down with Hosni Mubarak.' Oh Mona, I felt I was going to end oppression with my voice alone! I wasn't scared anymore."

She was moved by her own account and so was I. For a moment we stood in silence then I asked her to go on with her story, our story. All of the stories had become one big story, despite their differences in location, they all complemented each other.

"We walked together on Abdel Aziz Street and one of the girls who was with us started to talk to the shopkeepers and to ask them to join us. And people did! I heard one of them say, 'How can we just sit and watch when the women are on the street? Let's go, guys.' As soon as we got to Bab al-Louq, the teargas attack started. I can't even begin to tell you how much teargas they were showering us with. We were separated from each other and I was suffocating. I felt I was going to die. I had no oxygen in my lungs at all and so I told myself that this was the price of freedom. Some protestors I did not know helped me get back on my feet and I started to breathe very slowly again. Suddenly, I felt safe because I felt that those who helped me were like my brothers. Just as we were beginning to regroup and walk forward, the teargas canisters hit again. So we ran in different directions. I thought we would never reach Tahrir, but suddenly, I found myself in Tahrir, alone. At a distance, I could see the unbelievable amount of teargas that was being shot at Qasr al-Nil Bridge. One of the officers came up to me and began speaking to me in English. I couldn't understand why. When I ignored him, he spoke to me in Arabic, 'What are you doing here?' I said that I was watching. He said, 'You're not supposed to be here.' So

I asked him if he thought that he was getting decent food, if his kids were getting decent schooling, if he was satisfied with his life. He said 'No, but this is not the way to change things.' Then, I suddenly noticed that the officers had disappeared and the policemen found themselves abandoned. They just stood there looking lost and then they started to run. After a while, a small number of people began to enter the midan, but suddenly, an armored vehicle raced toward us, so we ran to avoid it. Then thousands of people arrived in the midan. The demonstrators who had been stuck on Qasr al-Nil Bridge made it to the midan, rolling burning barrels in front of them. The police ran away from them. It was very weird seeing the police run away from the people. I couldn't help laughing. It was actually very funny. Then I heard that they had set up a makeshift clinic at the corner of Tahrir Street, so I went to see how I might be useful. I saw wounded people drenched in dirt and blood. I think many of them died. I made a list of the medical supplies that were needed. I then saw people on a balcony and lights on the top floor of the building nearby, so I went up and knocked at their door and asked to use the bathroom and make a phone call. They welcomed me in and I told them about the injured. So they donated money and some of them came with me to buy medication from Manial. All of the pharmacies in Downtown were closed. We went back to the makeshift clinic. I had some leftover money, so I bought sandwiches and distributed them to people in the midan."

"Wow! What a girl! Why have I never taken you seriously!"

My sister smiled, despite being worn out and tired.

"But that's it! I can't do anything anymore. I need to go home."

"How are you going to go home now? Stay with us at Merit."

"I can't. I'm exhausted. I'll catch a ride in any car leaving from Downtown."

"We'll walk with you until you find a ride."

We walked to Midan Talaat Harb. There were citizens' checkpoints at all street entrances. The young protestors were holding wooden sticks and had placed empty tires in front of them as roadblocks. My sister signaled to a car in which there were two children. The family welcomed her in and offered to take her home, but they insisted on going to the museum first to make sure that it was safe. We told them that the museum was fine and that we had been there, but they still insisted on making doubly sure themselves. We smiled in appreciation for their concern.

"I will leave my sister with you."

"Don't worry. We will take her all the way home."

10

I Want to Sleep

The events of the day, as well as those of the previous ones, had done me in. I dragged my feet on the street. I wanted to sleep. I landed in Merit where the place was still packed and loud.

"Go inside and sleep with the girls," Mohamed Hashem said to me.

I went to the room but it was packed; so was the other room. I went back to the reception area and squeezed myself between friends. Some had fallen asleep, others were still talking, while others still were watching TV. I wanted to sleep, but in order for me to fall asleep, the place had to be quiet and dark. I got up and called a friend who lived on Champollion Street.

"Are you still up?"

"How can anyone get any sleep tonight? But I'm still going to try."

"Can I come and sleep over?"

"Of course."

I headed to Champollion Street like a sleepwalker. My friend opened the door.

"Unbelievable!"

"Yes, unbelievable it is."

We did not continue the conversation for we had seen everything with our own eyes.

She made the bed for me and went to her room.

"Goodnight."

"Goodnight."

"Or good morning, rather. It's almost dawn."

I shut the door, turned off the light, and lay in bed.

"The people demand the removal of the regime!"

I heard the people chanting incessantly in my ear. I smiled and was a bit put out at the same time. Please, not now, I want to sleep. But, to no avail, for the chanting besieged me like the buzzing of a bee. I tossed and turned trying to quieten my mind. But it would not stop. Scenes from the day mixed with stories from friends, images, and sounds. I placed the pillow over my head and shut my eyes. It still didn't work. I sat up and looked around me. What was I going to do now? I wanted to sleep. I lay down again and started to count: one, two, three.

"The people demand the removal of the regime!"

Again! It wasn't working; I couldn't sleep. I got up and went to the TV room. I flipped through the channels in search of a foreign film but I really didn't feel like watching a film. I flipped some more and watched scenes from the day's demonstrations. Suddenly, I felt that I didn't want to be alone. Since I couldn't sleep, it was best to be with my friends. I left my friend's house and went back to Merit.

11

Merit Publishing House at Dawn

"Where were you?"

"I went to a friend's house to try to get some sleep, but I couldn't sleep. So I came back to be with you."

"Would you like some tea?"

"Why not."

The commotion gradually died down. Everybody was tired. Someone turned off the TV, dimmed the light, and locked the door. I thanked him with all my heart. We sat around sipping our tea and smoking in peace. With this relative quiet and the dim lights, I fell asleep for a short while. I woke up to the sound of the doorbell.

"Could someone get the door, guys?"

"Whoever's closest to the door should get it."

"Some people are sleeping like the dead!"

Someone opened the door and two ghost-like figures walked in. We recognized them, of course; one of them turned on the light. We sat up alarmed by the appearance of the friends who had just arrived.

"Why do you look like that?"

"Where have you come from?"

"We were on Qasr al-Aini Street. There's a street battle going on down there."

One of them began to tell the story but was interrupted by one of us: "You were on Qasr al-Aini Street? Was there a demonstration out there?"

"There were at least fifty thousand people."

"So all the shooting we've been hearing was there?"

"It was a massacre. Teargas, bullets, and snipers. Many people died and countless have been injured."

"We thought they were just shooting to scare us so that no one would come near the Ministry of Interior."

"You should've seen it, this car with diplomatic plates ran over protestors. At least fifteen people died."

"Oh my God!"

"It's criminal. The car was going at full speed and just rammed into people. I was in front of it, but I quickly moved out of the way. It was a matter of a split second and it rammed people and ran them over. I was struck dumb. I still can't quite believe it."

We were equally flabbergasted and in complete disbelief. But someone quickly collected himself and said, "Catch your breath while I make another round of tea."

Our friends were too agitated, so they resumed their story:

"He could've just driven through and people would have made way for him. People were flying left and right in midair. People were dumbfounded. Some were screaming. We were all in disbelief and in tears. Some people tried to lift those who had fallen on the ground, some of them were not whole bodies any more: they were just parts and pieces of bodies. It was very difficult. Horrific."

"I can't believe that a normal human being would do that."

We were demoralized, so demoralized that we remained speechless and motionless. One of our friends came in with the tea tray and placed it in front of us.

"You have to retell the story in detail," one of us said finally.

After a moment of silence one of them resumed:

"I came from Maadi and I didn't think that people out there would join the demonstrations, but I joined a small group who were coming. We decided to take the Helwan Agricultural Road. That was a good decision because it goes through informal neighborhoods and we increased in number when people from the informal neighborhoods in Maadi, Dar al-Salam, and al-Zahra joined us. We were in the thousands. We marched until we reached the beginning of Qasr al-Aini Street where they started showering us with teargas. The march was dispersed: Some ran into the side streets in Garden City and others into the streets on the other side. Women on balconies threw us water, vinegar, and onions. We finally got to the offices of *Al-Masry Al-Youm* newspaper where I found many of my friends. One of them had been shot in the face. The people at *Al-Masry Al-Youm* were really great. The women came down with a big plastic bowl full of water, so that when the canisters landed, people could grab them and put them in the water. They also helped the protestors who fell. It was like a makeshift clinic. There was this great scene: Someone took the fire hose and opened the water on the front row of riot-police conscripts. They too attacked us with teargas and water, as we continued to shower them with the fire hose. We were laughing despite the shooting and the violence. Anyway, we made it through the first riot-police roadblock and into Qasr al-Aini Street again. We found another group of people who had come from Maadi and Old Cairo, and thousands on Qasr al-Aini. There were about fifty thousand people there."

He stopped to sip some of the tea that, by then, had gone cold. The other friend continued:

"I was in the second wave of demonstrators. We took the Corniche, and as soon as we got to Old Cairo, they started shooting teargas. To tell you the truth, we all felt betrayed because we had not come near them to begin with. We were just marching and minding our own business, and we were chanting, 'The people demand the removal of the regime.' The demonstrators retaliated by throwing stones at the police station, and after a while, some of the more fiery among us attacked the officers and the policemen. Suddenly, we saw an empty public bus; I don't know where it came from. It blocked the street down the middle of the Corniche, and then the driver turned it around and drove it right into the gate of the police station. It was positioned like a shield and the demonstrators started saying, 'Cross, cross.' And we did. As for the officers and the policemen, those who had time to run, did, and those who didn't got a good beating. We continued walking toward

Qasr al-Aini, but it was blocked. People paused for sunset prayer and then the attack started again: shooting, bullets, gas, you name it! Many were injured, but some of them went into the Qasr al-Aini Hospital and received first aid and came out and continued the fight. This fray went on for a long time. We were besieged for eight hours between the hospital and the parliament building and we had no idea what was happening in Tahrir. We heard that the army was already on the street. We didn't know whether they were with us or against us. We saw several tanks and armored vehicles drive down Qasr al-Aini Street. People climbed onto the tanks and kept telling the army officers 'They're attacking and killing us.' The army soldiers gently helped them down and the army officers reassured the people and told them not to worry. We kept following the tanks until we saw them enter Garden City and head toward the American Embassy. As soon as they had passed through, the shooting started again and there were snipers shooting from several directions. It got dark and we could no longer tell where they were attacking us from. A bit later, we saw more tanks and an armored vehicle. People cheered again and started chanting, 'The army and the people are one hand,' and the officers told us not to worry. As soon as they crossed the police roadblock, the shooting started again. Our numbers started declining . . . and then that car with diplomatic plates. I don't want to repeat that story."

He stopped, and the other friend picked up from there:

"There was a gas station that seemed to be under renovation and had been surrounded with a metal barrier. After the car had run over the people, some of the demonstrators dismantled the barrier, in a matter of seconds, and they took the sheets of wood that held it together and made roadblocks and shields. They used them to attack the police, who retreated. There was a pickup truck with a government license plate. People set it on fire and took the body of the truck and the tires and charged forward toward the first roadblock. More clashes. We sent the injured off in any private car that came by after we had blocked the ambulances from entering the street. The shooting would stop, then as soon as an ambulance showed up on the street, the shooting would increase. It was criminal. A man in a white Lancer, God bless him, kept shuttling back and forth to Qasr al-Aini Hospital to transport the injured. There was a nearby garage where people got water hoses and collected empty bottles. They went to the gas station and pumped the gasoline into the empty bottles and made Molotov cocktails. One of the really gutsy young demonstrators came and said to us, 'Guys, take your women away from here. It's gonna get wild now.' So we hid the women inside the entrance of a building where they could still watch. Our numbers decreased with the continuous attacks and because we couldn't make it to Tahrir and because it was already past midnight. Only small groups remained. They were the most determined to continue to the end. We started coordinating with each other: what we were going to do, where we were going to attack, from which direction—street-fighting strategies, you know. Some launched the attack, others threw the Molotov cocktails, while others still helped the injured. It was brilliant. But we still couldn't get through to Tahrir. So we decided to try to get there through Garden City, but we were a bit worried because we didn't know what to expect and we were afraid there might be snipers. Anyway, we took a shortcut and walked until we got to the Corniche near the Semiramis Hotel. It was quiet there and we saw people, with smiles on their faces, heading our way. We asked them about news from the midan and they told us that things were fine. They said that there hadn't been any shooting since sunset. 'Is the way clear to the midan?' we asked. 'Yes,' they said. 'Up to which point?' we asked. 'All the way to Tahrir,' they said. We couldn't believe our ears! Finally, we got into Tahrir and found that people were just hanging out. Then we came here."

"You've had a terrible day!"

"It was like being in a movie."

"We have to write these stories down, guys."

It was morning already. Our two friends who had arrived at dawn stretched out on the floor. We decided to rest for a while after their intense accounts. We turned off the lights and waited quietly for the curfew hours to end and for public transportation to resume.

Somebody laughed out loud.

"What's up? Didn't we say we'd rest a little?"

"It's just that I remembered a very funny scene. In the thick of the shooting, when we were by the gas station, there was a bank nearby with an ATM machine. Anyway, a couple of guys took one of the wooden poles they had dismantled at the station and kept trying to break the machine. Every once in a while people would come up and argue with them and drive them away, but they kept coming back and kept pushing and banging at the machine. It was hilarious! To think that they could bust open that metal machine with a wooden pole! Finally, the people caught them and gave them a good beating and drove them away. But the really funny part was when this old man, in shabby clothes, came up to me, saying, 'Keep an eye on that safe, son. People's money is in there.' I was a bit surprised because the guy looked like he had probably never laid eyes on a one-hundred-pound note. I couldn't get why he was so concerned about the machine."

More laughter.

"Remember the two stoned guys who came up to us at the kiosk in front of the offices of *Al-Masry Al-Youm*?"

"Yeah, they were really something! We saw these two guys who looked pretty stoned run toward the kiosk and then stop, look around, and ask, 'What's up guys? What's all this shooting?' So we told them that the police were shooting at us and asked them where they were coming from. One of them, who looked about forty years old, answered, 'We were just hanging out smoking a couple of joints when the canisters landed on us and the gas blinded us. So we figured our neighborhood was being attacked and got up to find out what was happening.' And when we started the attack on the first road block, they came with us. 'Let's do it guys,' they said."

Even more laughter.

"Oh, here's another scene I will never forget: A short while after the story with the car that had diplomatic license plates—when we were completely devastated and crying as people were collecting the dead bodies—a Fiat 128 drove by. The driver was listening to 'Ya habibti ya Masr' on his cassette player. We asked him to turn up the volume because we needed moral support. So, he stopped the car, opened the doors, and turned up the volume to full blast. People started crying and dancing. When it got to the line, 'He's never come to Egypt,' people shouted it out together, hysterically jumping up and down. Then we asked the same young man to drive up to the frontlines of the demonstrators to give them moral support. What a great guy! He kept driving up and down in the car replaying 'Ya habibti ya Masr'. I never felt the song this way before. It gave us goose bumps! It gave us strength and enormous determination. Really. Ya habibti ya Masr!"

Midan al-Tahrir: 7 a.m.

Some of us decided to go and check out the midan before the end of curfew hours at 8 a.m. We went to Qasr al-Nil Street. The NDP headquarters were still ablaze and the black smoke filled the morning sky; the fumes left no oxygen in the air. The army tanks and armored vehicles surrounded the midan and had closed off all its entrance points. At the edge of Midan Abdel Moneim Riyad, people were sleeping at the foot of the tanks and in between them; they were also sleeping at the entrances to shops and apartment buildings, on the asphalt, and inside the lawn area. Some were beginning to wake up while others were still sleeping. Some started to stroll around the midan and others started walking around briskly to stay warm. A charred police pickup truck sporting graffiti that read "Headquarters of the Filthy NDP" had been turned into a garbage dump.

I walked along with a group of friends, who were on their way to Hadayeq al-Qubba and Heliopolis, toward the metro station in Isaaf. There were charred police vehicles on the street. I took some photos as a souvenir. The traffic policemen had disappeared and people were organizing the traffic at the intersection of Ramsis and 26th of July Streets. The metro station was still closed. Taxis began to appear at the exit to Maarouf Street, but they were all full beyond capacity. I sat on the sidewalk as I could no longer stand. I wanted to be in my bed that very minute. Finally, the metro station opened its gates; people went straight through the gates to the tracks without buying tickets. There was no one at the ticket barriers. But I decided that I wanted to continue to be a good and responsible citizen, so I went to the ticket counter and bought myself a ticket. I collapsed on the first seat in the metro and tried to resist the total collapse of my body that would allow my drowsiness to make me miss my stop. I finally got home. My parents welcomed me with joy, love, and pride, as they had with my sister before me. My mother insisted that I must eat. But I wanted nothing but to be in my bed.

6
Saturday, January 29

I had imagined that as soon as I threw myself on my bed, in my own home, I would collapse and sleep. But no, that didn't happen. I kept tossing and turning in search of a comfortable position, but to no avail. My body began to ache after the beating I got on Wednesday. The people's chants to overthrow the regime echoed in my ears. An hour or two went by, but I still couldn't get any sleep. I wanted to go back to Tahrir. My sister and I got ready to go. My parents were in the living room watching television. We could hear women screaming for help on the TV that had not been turned off since the night before.

"Are you going out again?" my mother asked, with real surprise.

"Yeah."

"To do what? It's over. The president has appointed Omar Suleiman as vice president. He removed Ahmed Nazif and will give you Ahmed Shafiq."

"He can appoint whoever he wants. We don't want Hosni Mubarak himself. This is nonsense. All these guys are from the old guard. And what exactly do you mean by 'he will give you'? Aren't you on our side?"

"No, I'm not on your side. I'm with Hosni Mubarak."

"What?"

"Yes, I like Mubarak . . . . It's been thirty years."

"You like Mubarak and his thirty years . . . . What about our father?"

"Appointing a vice president just as he is almost out the door!" added my sister.

"Mama, we're off and we don't know when we'll be coming home. But don't worry, we'll spend the night at Merit or with friends in Downtown."

"Why don't you give the man a chance? Maybe he will change."

My father gently tried to discourage us from leaving.

"To tell you the truth, we don't believe him or his government. He really has to go now."

"They have been broadcasting the same statement all day on television, asking people to go back to their homes to protect them. Thugs are everywhere and people have been calling in asking for help. Police stations are on fire and prisoners have escaped."

"I have a feeling that the women asking for help are the wives of the officers. They're playing the part to scare the people. Just listen to them. Does that sound like the voice of a frightened woman who's being attacked by a thug? Come on! Anyway, this is exactly what happened in Tunisia. They opened up the prisons and released their thugs. But yesterday people organized citizens' checkpoints. Don't worry. Now, we need to get going."

"I just want to understand what exactly you intend to do."

"We'll stay with the people and whatever we can do, we will do."

"So you actually don't know exactly why you're going?"

"Baba, that's enough."

"No hope then?"

Laughing, I replied, "There will be hope. Egyptians are awake now. This in and of itself is an accomplishment. It is heroic."

"Won't you have lunch before you go?"

"Not important. Bye now."

"Call us."

"We will."

Once on the street, we bought enough from the bakery in our building to feed a lot of people. Everywhere we looked we could see the citizens' checkpoints guarding the entrances to the side streets. The street seemed narrower because of the huge rocks and tires that were placed down the middle so that cars had to slow down as they drove through. The young men were holding sticks and were checking people's licenses and trunks, exactly like the police, but more meticulously! We flagged down a cab.

"Tahrir, please?"

Without a word ,the driver gave us a dirty look, then took off with a wave of his hand.

"Thanks! We got the message!"

"Let's not say 'Tahrir.' Let's say 'Downtown,'" my sister suggested.

We stopped another cab.

"Downtown, please?"

He nodded positively.

We got in. The driver had gray hair and a beard.

"Good evening."

"Al-salamu alaykum."

He turned on the Qur'an, at full volume, so that my sister and I could no longer speak to each other.

"Could you please turn it down a little?"

He pretended to do so.

"Please turn it down a little. We want to talk about what's happening."

He ignored us, so we had to speak very loudly in order to hear each other. It was actually unbearable. The loudspeakers were right behind us, almost in our ears.

"Mister, this won't work! When the Qur'an is being recited, one should listen attentively."

"So listen," he replied, almost yelling at us.

"No, we want to talk."

"Get out of the car, then."

We were dumbfounded. He stopped and we got out. My sister and I looked at each other in shock, then we cracked up.

"Was that guy crazy or what?"

"It's his loss."

"Let's take the bus."

Almost all the passengers were earnestly talking politics—those for and those against the protests.

"They get paid and are given money and free meals from KFC, guys."

"They're beautiful young people who are protesting for their future."

I took note of the "money" and "meals from KFC." So that's what they were saying about us: we are traitors and mercenaries. I opened my bag and took out the baked goods that we had bought earlier and showed them to those who were saying that we ate meals from KFC. I was very angry at the unjust accusation. I began shouting, despite my completely broken voice:

"Look here, sir, does this look like a KFC meal? May God forgive you for what you're saying about us. We are protesting for the sake of Egypt, not for ourselves. We don't need anything but we are concerned about the situation in the country and the conditions of the poor."

"But on TV they've been saying that you are traitors and that you are taking money to destroy the country."

A woman turned around and looked at us suspiciously.

"That's Egyptian television, sir. Had you come yesterday and witnessed the hundreds of thousands that were there and all the shooting and violence against us, you would not have said this."

My voice was giving up on me so I stopped talking. A forty-year-old man took up the defense:

"Have you forgotten the ferry accident and all the people who died in it? Have you forgotten those who were burned alive inside the train to Upper Egypt? Do you like seeing all these children with cancer, those with kidney failure and Hepatitis C? Do you like all the stealing and corruption that surround us? Wake up Egyptians! Wake up!"

The man got off at Ramsis Station, and we got off at Isaaf and made our way to Merit through Downtown. The charred police vehicles were still there on Ramsis Street. The police had completely disappeared and people were organizing the traffic themselves. They were doing a much better job than the traffic police.

Merit had become the house of the nation. It was open to everyone whether they were friends or strangers. The television was always turned on for the news. Some watched, some talked, and others still wrote slogans and comments and drew caricatures on sheets of paper. One of our friends said that there had been several incidents of theft and looting:

"As I was on my way in the cab, just before the Shubra Tunnel, a couple of thugs wanted to stop us. I told the driver to keep going. I saw, with my own eyes, people inside the tunnel carrying refrigerators, washing machines, and television sets. Men, women, children, and even elderly people! A whole convoy of people carrying looted stuff!"

"But bear in mind that the stores that were attacked and looted were big and expensive stores like the ones at Arkadia Mall. No one tried to loot the small shops. People know who they are stealing from. It is also quite possible that the theft and looting was done by thugs working for the regime and the police and the Ministry of Interior—the same guys they use during elections. Remember the guys who were trying to loot the museum? They were from the police."

"Very possible. This happened in Tunisia too."

"What's really strange is that all this is happening while the army tanks are stationed only four or five hundred meters away."

"I really don't understand the army."

"No one understands a thing anyway."

I felt that I missed the midan. So my sister and I went off to take a tour. We were stopped at a checkpoint for our ID cards.

"We've just come from this building. The ID is in my bag upstairs."

"Okay, but this will be the last time. From now on, keep your ID cards in your pockets."

"Yes, sir!" we replied, laughing.

The crowds were much bigger. Some people had been there since the night before, while others had gone home in the morning and returned before noon. The smell of smoke and teargas was still in the air. There was unusual helicopter traffic in the skies. People started to put up tents in the central garden of the midan. Some groups were chanting, "The people demand the removal of the regime," and "Irhal, leave."

A group of young protestors sitting by KFC were drawing sketches of revolutionary scenes; others were spraying the army tanks, the doors of armored vehicles, the walls, and the metal roadblocks with "Down with Mubarak, the Dictator" and, "Leave, Mubarak." Another group was singing the songs of Sheikh Imam; a young man with shabby clothes stood in the middle of another group, improvising chants about Hosni Mubarak; another group sat apart reading the Qur'an; another group played soccer, children running around with them; and yet another group was sweeping the midan. I remembered the day of January 25. A new society was being born; a new spirit was in the making. There was a marvelous feeling that we had all become Egyptian again, real Egyptians; that this was our country and that we were not going to leave it or forsake it ever again.

We joined a large demonstration that was on its way to the TV Building in Maspero, chanting along with our broken voices,

"Irhal! Leave!"

We stopped chanting "The people demand the removal of the regime" because it further wore out our vocal cords, especially since it was in formal Arabic which we were not used to using for chants. One young man went against the group and started chanting, "The people demand the rescue of the regime." We were bent over laughing. Other people noticed the confusion of words in Arabic between "removal" and "rescue."

"It's 'removal,' not 'rescue,' boy!"

The young man laughed modestly and confusedly, displaying a row of broken teeth.

"I know, but that's how I heard it," he said, somewhat embarrassed.

"Removal, removal. The people demand the removal of the regime."

"Okay, got it. The people demand the removal of the regime," he repeated, taking great pains and articulating it as correctly as possible.

We continued marching past the army tanks and vehicles that were lined up by the museum. The chanting grew louder: "The army and the people are one hand!" We marched through Midan Abdel Moneim Riyad toward the TV Building. Both the street and the Corniche were blocked on both sides leading to the building. There were already large crowds. An army officer whose rank I didn't know and who had completely lost his voice was trying to talk to the people. One could tell that these were very simple people, just by looking at them. We stopped to listen. It was obvious that the conversation had been going on for some time already, and had been repeated with several groups. The officer was asking them:

"Why do you want to enter the Television Building?"

The people didn't really have an answer.

"We want the removal of the regime."

"People, the curfew will begin in a little while. You should go now and come back tomorrow. Come every morning and leave by the end of the day."

Some started to laugh sarcastically.

"You want us to go now and then come back every day? So we can't ever get in? No, we will not leave."

"All right then, stand for as long as you want. No one is going into the building."

"This is really an absurd conversation," I said to my sister.

"Really funny," she laughed. "Go home and come back tomorrow!"

"But actually, the officer is right. What are these people going to do inside the building when they can't even speak properly?"

We went back to the midan and then to Merit to rest for a while and exchange accounts and stories.

"So, what news from the Cairo Book Fair? Did Mubarak go to the opening or did he ditch the whole thing?"

"Yeah, didn't *al-Ahram* confirm on Thursday that he would go to the opening today?"

"Forget about that. Here's the latest joke: Mubarak was watching the demonstrations and could hear the people chanting for the removal of the regime. He said to himself: 'Thank God, my name isn't Regime.'"

"That's a good one."

"Here's another good one: When Mubarak went to heaven he met Sadat and Abdel Nasser. They both wanted to know how he came to join them. So they asked him, 'Assassination like Sadat or poison like Nasser'? He lowered his head and said, 'No, Facebook.'"

"That's a great one!"

"Very funny."

"I can't believe the amount of jokes making the rounds already!"

The laughter did not last for long. By evening, we heard that there were snipers around Midan Abdel Moneim Riyad and on the rooftop of the Ramsis Hilton and that there had been many deaths and injuries. Reports from Qasr al-Aini Street confirmed that the shooting was still going on and that there were more deaths and injuries.

"How can all this happen in the presence of the army?"

We were depressed. All we could do was return to the midan.

We avoided going through Midan Abdel Moneim Riyad and headed straight to Qasr al-Aini Street. We could hear live bullets and people shouting, "Make way, make way!" A number of motorbikes raced by: the driver, another person behind him, and the limp body of a third person between them—someone either injured or dead, who had lost limbs, or was drenched in blood.

I placed my hand over my mouth, but a gasp still escaped from between my lips, and I began to cry. We ran behind the motorbikes all the way to the small mosque that had been transformed into a make-shift clinic the day before. People were yelling, "Mind the blood," others were screaming, "We need doctors quickly, guys."

Oh God, I beg your forgiveness, your forbearance, your mercy. Why is this happening? Oh God, I beg your forgiveness, your forbearance, your mercy. Why all this all this happening? Oh God, this is so unjust. Oh God, this is so unjust.

There was only one shabby ambulance. The mosque was over-crowded with those who had been injured. Inside, the doctors could not keep up with the number of injured people who were being brought to the mosque after Qasr al-Aini Hospital refused to admit them. My sister made a list of the medication and medical supplies that were urgently needed. We started to call friends and acquaintances to pro-vide the needed supplies. Those who knew doctors contacted them. Many expressed their immediate willingness to come and help.

"What happened?"

One of the eyewitnesses began to tell the story:

"Our neighbor died at Qasr al-Aini Hospital today. He was a won-derful young man, about twenty years old. He was shot last night at the demonstration on Qasr al-Aini Street. As the funeral marched toward Tahrir, we carried the coffin with his family and friends and we were shot at by the police. We hadn't come near them. The con-frontations had started again in the area surrounding the Ministry of Interior and the Parliament. Large groups of protestors arrived with Molotov cocktails and burning tires to avenge the death of their relatives last night: those who were killed by the snipers, in face-to-face confrontations, and those who had been run over by the white car with diplomatic plates. Hundreds had died and several hundred others were injured."

"Have mercy, dear God!"

"Okay, no one is to go anywhere near there anymore. That's enough!"

"But what about the people who lost their children and brothers in cold blood? What will they do? Yesterday, they swore that they would avenge their children today."

"I understand. But you can't just attack the Ministry of Interior with Molotov cocktails when they have real weapons."

"God save us!"

I wandered around the midan with a heavy heart. I bumped into a friend who was on his way back from the Ministry of Interior. He looked dazed.

"I saw an officer with my own eyes open fire. He had a machine gun and fired randomly, right and left. With my own ears, I overheard the communication signal from the officer's wireless: 'Long live the regime of Hosni Mubarak!' The day before, the signal had been, 'Long live Egypt.' I also heard it then."

And then he walked away.

I went back to Merit and sat down quietly. The stories had already been told so there was no reason to go through the pain again. I watched the news on the TV screen: Demonstrations in almost all Egyptian cities, demonstrations and marches in solidarity with Egyptians in several Arab and foreign cities, protests against the government in Jordan, calls for help against thugs in different places in Cairo and other cities, the burning down of NDP offices and police stations in various governorates.

I was exhausted. I couldn't even remember when I had last slept. I jumped in my seat when I heard warnings that thugs on the streets were raping girls. Our friends asked us not to move around alone. I suddenly remembered my sister. I started looking for her among those who were at Merit. I couldn't find her. I called her.

"Where are you?"

"I'm in the mosque."

"What are you doing there? You're not a doctor!"

"I'm writing a list of the supplies and calling up doctors."

"Please come back. The thugs are everywhere on the streets raping girls."

"Don't worry. I'm with lots of people."

"Who are these people? Do I know them?"

"They're doctors, Mona."

"Please come back. I have enough worries already."

"Okay."

I waited for her, but she did not come. More talk about rape. I called her again and shouted at her to come back. We were disconnected. I asked a couple of friends to accompany me to the mosque, so I could bring my sister back. Almost everyone on the street in the vicinity of the midan was armed with a stick. I could no longer tell the thugs from the citizens' checkpoints. We got to the alleyway where the makeshift mosque clinic was located. It was very crowded. Someone was addressing the people standing around through an amplifier, asking them to make way for the doctors so that they could come through and do their work.

"Those who have no reason to be here should leave."

"Excuse me but my sister is inside. May I come in to get her?"

"Is she injured?"

"No, she's helping out."

"What does she look like?"

"I don't know what she's wearing. She's not veiled, she's rather petite, and she looks like me."

"Come in and show her to me and I will get her for you."

"Thank you."

I made my way through the crowd. As I was doing so, someone groped my breast. I was horrified. I yelled at him: "You bastard!" I couldn't identify him in the crowd and in the dark. By the time I got to the entrance of the mosque, I was fuming. Bodies were stretched out or curled up on the ground; there was blood everywhere. It was a terrible sight. A group of young men and women surrounded the doctors. I found my sister with them. I called out to her.

"That's her!"

"Okay. Just a moment, I'll get her."

"Please stay with me. There are some shady guys in the crowd."

I walked out and waited with the friends who had accompanied me. My sister finally came out.

"Why are you so worried about me all of a sudden?"

"Listen Maha, they've been talking about rape over and over again. I can't leave you here."

95

"So you're playing mom?"

"I don't want to play mom, but I'm the older sister, and unfortunately, I feel responsible."

"I'm not a little girl. I can look after myself."

"I'm sorry. You can go wherever you want but with people I know."

She didn't answer me.

We went back to Merit and sat in different spots. Cigarette smoke filled the air and I knew that my sister would not be able to take that. She began to look tired, so I took her to a friend's house on Bustan Street and left her there. I felt relieved. I went back to Merit. We started making sandwiches like the day before. I helped out with the distribution, then I asked a couple of friends to accompany me to Champollion Street to spend the night with a friend. We talked for a while and then my friend went to sleep. I tried to sleep too but I just couldn't. I watched TV for a bit and then turned it off. I left the house and quietly shut the door behind me. At this rate, I was going to end up having a nervous breakdown. I walked briskly, looking around me all the time. I went through the alleyway beside Le Grillon and straight back to Merit.

"You're back again!"

"I can't sleep."

Some people were sleeping already, some were watching TV, some had gone to the midan and come back, and some were chatting. Finally, the voices died down, the TV was turned off, and silence reigned.

Suddenly, we heard the thundering chant, "The people demand the removal of the regime!"

We jumped up.

"What's happening?"

"Don't be scared. It's the ring tone of my cell phone."

"To Hell with you! Who needs this now?"

"How did you do that?"

"I recorded it during the demonstration."

"I want that ring tone too!"

7
Sunday, January 30

Morning

It was morning already. The curfew hours had ended. I wanted to go home, but I didn't have the energy to walk to the metro station at Isaaf. If only I could sleep for two hours. I went into the room where the girls were sleeping. I woke one of them up: "Get up. It's already nine o'clock. I want to sleep a little."

She got up and the others followed suit. I lay on the floor. Everyone was getting up and the commotion started all over again. After a while, Mohamed Hashem called me for breakfast, "Get up. We have fuul and hot taamiya for breakfast."

"Let me just sleep for an hour."

But I love taamiya. I got up and had some. I had some coffee and regained some of my energy. I went down to the midan with friends. Helicopters were circling in the sky. I heard people saying that the Ministry of Defense had issued a statement, saying it would come down hard on lawlessness on the streets.

"Guys, where do we stand in all of this, in their view?"

"I don't know. Maybe they're talking about the thugs."

I was suddenly overtaken by fear. I went back to Merit and called my sister.

"Come quickly. The Ministry of Defense said they're going to attack."

"What are you talking about? That's nonsense."

"Hurry up. We have to go home."

"I'm having breakfast."

"What do you mean breakfast? I just told you they're going to attack us. Come quickly."

But she dragged her feet. I called her again, screaming, "Hurry up. I'm leaving now."

And I did. She caught up with me on the way to Isaaf metro station. She tried to stop me, so I yelled at her as I continued walking, "You're irresponsible. Think about Mama and Baba. Do you want me to have to tell them Maha died? Have some pity on them."

"Why all this drama? It's clear you didn't get any sleep. That's why you're behaving like this."

"Go die, if you want to die. Don't come with me."

I walked faster and she followed.

"Get out of here. I told you that I don't want you to come with me."

She didn't reply and continued to follow me. We got to the metro station. I got into the carriage, still mumbling, with my sister by my side, smiling but not answering me. People were watching us curiously. She remained behind me until we got home.

"I followed you home because I wanted to make sure that you didn't collapse on the way. I'm going back to Tahrir. And don't tell Mama and Baba that I came all the way back here. Get some sleep. You need to sleep."

I went up.

"Where's your sister?"

"In Tahrir."

"Why didn't she come with you?"

"I'm not responsible for her. I'm tired. I want to sleep."

Afternoon

The saying goes: Sleep is health and strength. I woke up after four hours of deep sleep just before curfew. I felt optimistic and hopeful. My mother insisted that I have lunch before leaving. I ate what she had prepared quickly and asked her about my father.

"He went to Tahrir."

"What! Baba went to Tahrir? To do what?"

"He went to check out what was happening and look for your sister."

"Look for my sister? Through all these crowds? It's good that he went though, so he can be reassured and participate, even with just a stroll around the midan."

I suddenly realized how unpleasant I had been to my sister and was ashamed of myself. I left in a hurry. I went to the bakery downstairs. Almost all the baked goods had disappeared, except for some cookies.

"What's going on, guys? Is there a famine in Egypt?"

"People are scared."

"What are they scared of? This is not a war! It's ridiculous that people should be stocking up like this."

"It's the same with pharmacies. They've been cleaned out."

"God help us!"

"Okay, please give me two kilograms of cookies."

I stopped a cab.

"Downtown, please?"

The driver nodded.

"Could you please turn on the news?"

"I only listen to the Qur'an."

"But I'm going to Tahrir and I need to know what's happening."

"I only listen to the Qur'an."

I cut it short:

"Let me off here, please."

I got off where the citizens' checkpoint was stationed. I was in complete disbelief.

"What's wrong? What's this frown on your face?" one of the young men asked me jokingly.

So I told him what had happened with the cab driver.

"Don't be upset. We'll get you a cab and tell him to turn on the news for you."

A private car, with a man and a woman in their thirties inside, stopped. The young man checked the driver's license and the trunk. Then he asked the driver, "Are you going to Tahrir?"

"Yes."

"Could you take the lady with you?"

"Absolutely!"

"Say 'bougie' when you get to the next checkpoint."

"What should I say?"

"'Bougie.' That's the code so that they don't search you again."

It was very similar to what actually takes place at police checkpoints on the desert road. I smiled. The young man was playing the part of the police officer quite seriously. We began talking on the way to Tahrir. The young man and woman were quite recently married. They lived in the Rehab compound. They had a little girl whom they left with the young man's mother. They had joined the demonstrations the first day. I was surprised.

"We're not part of this for ourselves. We're doing this for our daughter and the baby that is on the way. We are participating so that their future may be better," said the young woman.

"My father has secured my future. He gave me a good education, so I was able to find a good job. I am a computer programmer. My father bought me an apartment and secured a lot of good things for me. But I won't be able to do the same for my children. I want my country to be clean for their sake. I want to be able to raise them properly and give them a good education so that when they grow up they can find jobs and homes," the husband said, as we drove through several checkpoints.

"Bougie."

"Go ahead."

We got to the end of the street.

"Bougie."

"Bougie?"

"It's the code."

"No, that was for the other end of the street. Your license, please."

The young man finished searching; he smiled and raised the front windshield wipers. We were puzzled.

"This is your passport for the next leg."

We smiled back.

"You're pretty organized about this! Bravo, guys!"

We got to Tahrir and were surprised to see that an F16 airplane was rocking the skies over the midan, flying so low that it almost hit the rooftops of the buildings. We were shocked. Nailed to the ground, we stood watching it above us. Suddenly, the demonstrators started chanting, "Hosni has gone cuckoo! Hosni has gone cuckoo!" We were bent over with laughter at the chant. The airplane disappeared. I said goodbye to the young man and woman and went to Merit. My sister was making tea for the people in the midan. I apologized to her and we agreed that each of us would look after herself and that it wasn't necessary for us to always move together. Actually, I didn't want to know where my sister was, nor did I want to know what she was doing. I didn't want to be worried about her and then start bossing her around without really meaning to.

Merit had been transformed into a workshop for the creative arts. There were sheets of paper, markers, and revolutionary posters everywhere. People took them to display in the midan. I remembered how hopeful I felt when I got up that morning. I started humming Fayruz's song to myself, "Yes, there is hope." I took a sheet of paper and wrote, "Now I Can Get Married and Have Kids. There is Hope in the Future. Yes, There is Hope." My friends laughed at what I had written.

"It's not going to work for you, Mona, no matter what you do!"

"It doesn't really have to happen but it's important that I feel this way. Before January 25, I would have never thought about it. Have kids and raise them on the street or go beg for their food or steal? I wouldn't want my kids to grow up in this corrupt environment."

I took my sign and went off to the midan. I discovered that some of the young protestors were holding signs that were similar to mine: "I Want to Get Married," "I Want to Get Married and Have Kids." I greeted them and we laughed together as they proposed to me.

"Sorry, I'm a bit old for you guys."

I took a look around the midan. There were long queues in front of the toilets by Omar Makram Mosque, but no one was complaining. People were chatting and smiling. There was no pushing or fighting, no swearing or cussing. I marveled at Egyptians. What a change! People gathered in the gardens: some were singing, some were resting, children were playing, and others were holding up signs and walking around the midan like me. There was an art exhibit in front of KFC and a young man with a laptop and two loudspeakers playing Abdel Halim Hafez's revolutionary songs of the 1960s: "Ours is a revolution for freedom and social justice," "I swear by its sky and its lands." He also played Shadia's "Ya habibti ya Masr," and "Bismillah, Allahu Akbar." We sang along passionately.

In the evening, one of our activist friends took the initiative of organizing a friendly soccer game on Talaat Harb Street between the people and the army. The goal itself was the angle between two army tanks that had been positioned to block the street. Both teams played energetically; the audience cheered, "The army and the people are one hand!" The game ended with the victory of the people over the army so they cheered: "We are the people!"

I went back to Merit and we started making sandwiches for distribution in the midan. Graphic artist Ahmed al-Labbad walked in with a beautiful painting.

"Where have you been?"

"I've been with the citizens' checkpoints for two days."

"Show us what you painted."

He placed the painting in front of us. We cracked up laughing. He had painted a caricature of Mubarak; he had put a barcode across it and had written underneath "Expired on January 25, 2011." There was another painting of an airplane and a flight ticket with a departure stamp that read "Departure date: January 2011."

"It's fantastic!"

"Absolutely amazing!"

We went back to making the sandwiches amid much laughter and chatter. We took them to the midan, and within minutes, we had finished the distribution. I stayed in front of KFC where they were playing revolutionary songs and dancing in a circle. They played the anthem "Bismillah, Allahu Akbar," which is one of my favorite songs. I feel blessed every time I hear it. The young protestors started to dance in a dabka-like circle. I found myself propelled into it. They made space for me to join and widened the circle. As I danced to the dabka steps, one of the young men came up and danced with me, without touching me.

"Bismillah! Allahu Akbar!" we shouted, raising our arms up high and jumping up and down as we danced.

I stopped before the end of the song, completely out of breath.

"Why did you stop?" asked one of the young men sweetly.

"I'm tired. It's age, you know."

He smiled and said, "Okay, take a break and come back."

"Your wish is my command!"

And so, I took a short break. The protestors replayed the song, so I joined them once more in the circle. This went on for several rounds, till dawn. When I got tired, I stepped out of the circle and sat on the sidewalk. As I sat there, I bumped into a friend; he got tea and joined me, and we started telling stories. My friend then went to the room he had rented in a small hotel off Tahrir and I returned to Merit. And of course, first come, first served: there was no space to sleep. I took off my coat and spread it on the floor and tried to get some sleep despite the noise and the cold. The young man in charge of the office next door to Merit came by and, seeing me and another girl in this uncomfortable position, invited us to sleep in his office. We thanked him for his kindness and went over. We lay on the floor till morning

8
Monday, January 31

I woke up feeling tired, having spent the night on the floor without a cover. I had some bread and cheese and leftovers from dinner the night before that I found at Merit. I then had coffee. It was exactly what I needed. I went for a stroll in the midan with friends. Those who had spent the night there told us that a couscous handcart had arrived in the midan during the early hours of the morning and was greeted jubilantly by everyone. People hurried toward it and organized themselves in queues without fighting for their turn. The owner of the cart and his assistant worked nonstop until the huge couscous pots were wiped clean before everyone could get a portion.

"Great! So now we know that tomorrow there will be more couscous."

"Don't worry. In a while there will be a fuul cart and a liver sandwich cart as well in the midan."

"I hope so. I'm sick and tired of cheese sandwiches."

"But you have to wake up very early and wait in the midan."

We laughed and waited for the other handcarts, that had become our saviors, to show up.

I greeted friends and strangers who were no longer strangers. I don't quite know when it happened but two TV screens had been set up next to Hardee's and had been connected to one of the lampposts in the midan. They were both tuned to Al Jazeera so that people in the midan could follow the news. Revolutionary songs were still being played near KFC; the makeshift clinics had multiplied in different spaces around the midan; the army and the people were still "one hand"; and the citizens' checkpoints were still doing their job with the help of army personnel. One of the members of the coordination committee asked me to help checking the women at the entrance point of the midan from Talaat Harb Street. I was more than happy to help and headed toward the area he had signaled. I stood with a young man and an army soldier. I checked ID cards, verified the line that said "occupation," searched women's bags for sharp objects like nail files or scissors, and I gently felt their head veils lest these objects be hidden inside them. When the number of women decreased, I helped search the men. It suddenly dawned on me that I finally had the chance to harass the men and to show them how it felt when they harassed us. I grabbed a young man in a heavy sweater and said to him jokingly, "Finally, I get a chance to feel you up!"

The young man was shocked and tried to protect his body from my hands.

"No, no, no!"

The young man, the soldier, and I started laughing.

"See? It really isn't fun."

I know that the percentage of unemployment in Egypt is very high, but when I verified the occupation on the young men's ID cards, I was heartbroken and shocked. Most of the IDs said "Obtained a degree in . . . ." And most of those were from very mediocre schools. When I asked them about their jobs the answer was "unemployed" or "whatever I can find."

I was exhausted, having been on my feet for such a long time, so I asked to take a short break and then come back again. I returned to Merit because I needed to use the bathroom and rest for a while. Everyone was following, with distaste, the new members of government being sworn in by Hosni Mubarak.

"Shame! Gaber Asfour accepted the portfolio of the minister of culture."

"The seduction of power!"

"He could have declined for health reasons. And he is actually not well. To tell you the truth, I no longer respect him. I used to like him a lot. I am even thinking of calling him to ask him why he is doing this to himself. But I'm too disgusted. This will be his downfall—the mistake of his life."

I was angry at Gaber Asfour. I was saddened by him and for him. He had done great damage to his personal history as an intellectual, as an academic, and as a civil servant.

I went back to the midan. I looked out in the direction of the museum and my eyes spotted my cousin. I couldn't believe it. I ran toward him, through the crowds, in complete disbelief. My cousin is a couple of years older than me. He had left Egypt after high school. He had married and gone to Australia several years ago. He had two beautiful children. He saw me and came toward me with open arms. We hugged each other tightly.

"When did you come back?"

"On the 29th. I went to see your mother and came straight to the midan."

"Look at this!"

"I can't believe it. I'm so happy."

"See, there is still hope."

"You know, Mona, I'm beginning to think of coming back to Egypt. Do you know how long I've been away?"

"I know. It's been almost twenty-five years."

He introduced me to his friends from Old Cairo, then he showed me photos of his children.

"Where are you based in the midan?"

"I move around, but you will most probably find me at the entrances to Talaat Harb, Champollion, and Qasr al-Nil streets, and at Merit. How about you?"

"My friends and I have decided to stay near the museum."

"Great, let's meet up later."

I went back to the corner of Talaat Harb Street and resumed my duties at the checkpoint at the entrance to the midan. I smiled at all of those who were arriving.

"Sorry, guys. No hard feelings about body searching. It's for your own safety and for the safety of those inside."

Actually, no one was upset by it. On the contrary, they were all very cooperative. They had their ID cards in hand and they opened their bags beforehand in preparation for the search.

My favorite song was being played again: "Bismillah, Allahu Akbar."

I asked a girl nearby to take my place at the checkpoint, while I went to dance in the circle that was being formed. I snatched Egypt's flag from one of the bystanders and held it up high, as I danced dabka in the middle of the circle with the young guys. This song gave me a lot of energy. They played it again. Another girl joined the circle, so the young men got more excited about dancing and so did we. "Bismillah . . . ." I prayed that God would grant us victory and help us through this moment as he helped us cross the Bar Lev Line to the Sinai in 1973. "Please God, I really didn't want to ask you for victory against other Egyptians, but what can we do?"

A call for the first million-man march the next day—Tuesday—was circulating in the midan. Al Jazeera also announced the call. There was news that roads surrounding Cairo were being blocked and that the train service had stopped. Despite that, or maybe because of it, the demonstrations continued in most cities and governorates, as well as in Arab countries and around the world.

I returned to Merit late at night, completely exhausted. I grabbed something to eat and lay on the floor like the night before. Once more, the young neighbor from the office next door to Merit let me into the office with the other girls who were still around. He gave us the key so we could lock ourselves in. I lay on the carpet and covered myself with my coat.

"Thank you, dear. You're very kind."

"You're welcome. Have a good night."

The young man went to join his colleagues at the citizens' checkpoint. The girls and I chatted until our words ran out. We slept like logs.

9
Tuesday, February 1, The First Million-Man March

Thousands of Egyptians of all shapes, colors, classes, and ages flocked to the midan early in the morning. Some were carrying Egypt's flag; others were holding different signs, many of which were very funny:

"Mubarak, Fly Away Now."

"Leave, Thank You!"

"Saudi Arabia Awaits You."

"Mubarak, Sorry, You Have No More Credit."

"Leave, I Want to Live."

"I Want the Internet Back."

"I Want Hashish."

Groups of people were chanting, "The people demand the removal of the president." I headed toward my new location at the Talaat Harb Street entrance to the midan. I joined two girls who were searching women. We divided the work among us: one checked ID cards or school IDs, one checked handbags, and the third did the body search. Some of my friends came through; they showed their IDs and joked around with me.

"You know us."

"No cutting corners! Come on, out with your IDs!"

I saw the army officer I had tried to flirt with the night the army had arrived in the midan standing on top of a tank and addressing the people through a loudspeaker: "If you spot anyone in a military uniform that is different from what we are wearing, you must hand him over to us." I suddenly realized that the uniforms of the soldiers and officers were different from the ones they had been wearing for the past few days, but I had thought that this was just a routine change. News spread that there had been thefts of military uniforms and that we should be watchful of infiltrators among the protestors. I noticed a group of men with a blue flag advancing through the men's queue at the checkpoint. Protestors from Suez! I ran toward them and greeted them.

"Welcome to the men of Suez!"

I went back to my position and found that other girls had taken over the search duties, so I decided to take a walk in the midan. I found my sister distributing tea. I extended my hand to her jokingly: "Can I have some?"

"Go and make some for yourself. This is for the people in the midan."

"I'm in the midan, too, you know. Where did you make the tea?"

"Upstairs at Pierre's place."

"Who's Pierre?"

"I don't know his last name. He's this big guy who lives on the ninth floor up there. That's where I went last Friday and they gave me money to buy medical supplies and food."

She pointed out the Misr Travel building with a tilt of her head; it was the first building on Talaat Harb Street.

"Oh, it's Pierre Sioufi."

She left me and went to give out more tea. I walked around, among these thousands of people. I had only seen such huge crowds on television during the pilgrimage. Many others were strolling around the midan like me: they smiled at each other, they apologized if they accidentally pushed each other, they greeted one another and exchanged jokes and condolences, and they stopped to talk about current events. Someone behind me was shouting on his cell phone as I continued walking:

"You will get to a small midan and you will see a statue in front of you. Go straight, past the first tank, the second tank, and the third tank, then, make a left. You will find another tank to your left. Cross over to the other side and you will find me standing by the scaffold."

These were the strangest directions I had ever heard in my life. I laughed heartily and turned around.

"We're not from Cairo," he said. "We don't know the street names. We came this morning from Sharqiya. Many others are on their way."

"Greetings to the people of Sharqiya! It's great to have you in the midan."

I looked up at the effigy dangling from a rope between two traffic lights. I had not seen it before. I continued my tour of the midan: a young woman with long hair stood in the midst of a group singing,

"Pull yourself together Egypt. Freedom is being born."

The group chanted along with her. A man in his fifties in a gallabiya stood in the middle of another circle singing madih, originally meant in praise of the Prophet Mohamed, that he was improvising to praise the revolution:

"For the sake of the Prophet, for the sake of the Prophet, take Mubarak, please."

The group laughed, applauded, and sang along. Near Hardee's, there was a full-blown sound system with a large television screen that was donated by one of the shop owners. Fervent speeches, and revolutionary poetry, a lost and found table full of ID cards and cell phones, and another with various cell phone chargers for those who needed to recharge their phones. There were several tea stands that had been set up. Tents with various signs filled the central and side gardens of the midan: "Resort of Happiness," "Resort of the Revolution," "Resort of Freedom." There were all kinds of people and families. The midan was life itself.

I went back to the entry point at Talaat Harb Street and joined the coordination committee that helped organize people's entry into the midan so that they would not block the space between the two tanks stationed there. The numbers were close to a million and the chanting was increasingly intense,

"The people demand the removal of the regime!"

"The people demand the removal of the president!"

"Leave!"

One girl was chanting very excitedly and loudly into my ear so I turned my head away from her,

"Not so close to my ear, please."

She didn't seem to understand what I meant.

"I'm chanting for the revolution," she said.

"Yes, I know but not in my ear. Is this your first day?"

"Yes," she responded proudly.

"This explains the great enthusiasm. I've been here since January 25. So I'm really tired. Keep chanting but further away from me."

The enthusiastic girl laughed and turned to face the other side of the midan rather than the direction of the tank and continued chanting as loud as she could: "The people demand the removal of the regime!"

I offered cigarettes to the protestors who were around me. They took them gratefully. A woman came by and offered us dates, insisting that we take some.

"No, thank you! Give them to the others."

There was plenty of food and drink for everyone: people were handing out juice, water, and sandwiches. But I had gotten used to surviving on the bare minimum, so I ate very little. Every once in a while, a group of my friends passed by. We would hug and kiss each other. I could sense how surprised my fellow committee members were and I could see the smiles on their faces. One of them mustered the courage to ask me, "Are all these people your relatives?"

"No, they are my friends."

I laughed and so did he.

I stood on the metal roadblock between the two army tanks, so I could get a better view of the midan. In the midst of the crowds, a large group of protestors was circling the square with a very long Egyptian flag while chanting:

"He must leave! We won't leave!"

I liked that chant a lot. It sounded very Egyptian. Despite the power of the Tunisian chant, "The people demand the removal of the regime," it was heavy because it was in formal Arabic. When I chanted it I felt like I was a member of the militias of Hizbollah. But, "He must leave; we won't leave," had more of an Egyptian spirit to it, so I swayed my body as I repeated it. I excused myself from the committee and made my way through the crowds to see who the group chanting was. It was the Ultras. I knew it! This great chant could not have come from ordinary people like us, or of our age bracket. I joined this young group and so did many others who were older and we all chanted fervently and rhythmically along with them,

"He must leave! We won't leave!"

Everyone was laughing. The Ultras radiated joy. Then they chanted, "Leave, ho, ho," several times. Then, in a highly improvised moment, as a woman was explaining the chant to her little son and saying, "'Leave' means 'go,'" a young man beside her added,

"Leave means go! In case you didn't know!"

Amazing creativity! That was how another brilliant chant emerged.

"Leave means go! In case you didn't know!"

The protestors were circling the midan with the long Egyptian flag raised above their heads, chanting both chants alternately with everyone else joining in. I spent the whole day moving around the midan, from one entry point to another, helping out with the coordination committee.

Throughout the day, I heard people on the phone to each other: "They say that they will cut off the electricity and leave the midan in the dark."

"They say that they will cut off the water supply."

"They say that they will send thugs."

"They say that . . . ."

So I asked, "Who is 'they,' guys?"

But the answer was just, "They say . . . ."

We heard that the president was going to address the nation again. What was he going to say? Was he going to step down? I bumped into a friend who has a banana plantation, and he told me that a pickup truck would be coming to the midan the next morning with bananas and that he wanted to be able to bring it into the midan through the Mohamed Mahmoud Street entrance. We went together to Lieutenant Mohamed to ask for permission.

"No problem. So long as the food is decent. We don't want people saying that the army is distributing bad food supplies."

"Don't worry, sir. These are organic bananas."

I went back to Merit to rest a little and to listen to the speech that was expected at any minute. I squeezed myself between two people and stretched out my legs. I suddenly remembered a scene with a police officer at a checkpoint at Saint Catherine's on my way back from Mount Sinai. I was in a cab, in the backseat so I could stretch out my legs. The officer asked the driver, "Any foreign passengers in the car?" It was a strange question as I was the only one in the cab.

"No, she's Egyptian," the driver said.

The officer looked at me in disgust and I looked back at him in bewilderment.

"You've just come down the mountain, right?"

I nodded.

"So that's why you have your feet up in my face at the checkpoint."

I was dumbstruck.

He signaled to the driver to get going.

Time went by and we were still waiting for the speech.

Does it have to be like this every time? Do we have to wait around again for hours to hear His Excellency?

I was beginning to lose my energy; I felt tired and I had a headache. The place was packed and noisy and so was the midan. I didn't know where to go. I needed some quiet even if just for an hour. I decided to go to see friends in Abdeen. There was a padlock at the entrance of their building. I didn't know what to do. I had lost my contact list on the old cell phone. I could see light in my friends' apartments, so I tried to call out to them from downstairs. Nothing but groaning came out; my vocal chords were completely shot. I just stood there. I didn't have the energy to go back to Merit or anywhere else. I looked around me. Tanks and armored army and military police vehicles. There was very little light and standing there made one look quite suspicious. I tried to find my voice.

"Hey!"

A man turned around and looked at me.

"I'm friends with Mr. Mohamed and Mr. Mustafa on the third floor. Could you please unlock the door?"

The man looked at me suspiciously. So I added in a completely broken voice: "I'm also friends with Mrs. Leila on the second floor."

He unlocked the door and let me in. I thanked him and went up.

"You're lucky! We were just about to have dinner."

"I just need to rest for an hour."

"Have something to eat first. I made some lentil soup."

"Lentil soup! Perhaps I am hungry after all."

I tried to rest for a while but was afraid I'd miss the historic moment—the speech should be any minute now. I got up and sat with my friends in front of the screen feeling exhausted.

"Do you want coffee?"

"I've been drinking coffee all day."

"Some Scotch? Shall I make you a drink?"

"That's it—I need something strong."

My mood improved and I felt re-energized. I decided I was going to spend the night in the midan.

"Do you have a mattress and blanket that I can borrow?"

"Let me check."

My friend gave me a mattress and a white bedcover.

"You don't have to return them."

"Let's go and listen to the speech in the midan."

"Let's do it!"

I carried the mattress and my friend carried the bedcover. We met a group of young men on the way who looked like thugs for sure. One of them came up to me and shouted in my ear, "Say yes to Mubarak."

I retreated a little and said, "Yes, and yes again, and for the third time, yes to Mubarak. Why ever not, brother?"

"What a coward you are!" my friend said laughing at me.

"A coward? Didn't you see what they looked like?"

We got to the midan. Thousands were gathered around the TV screens that were hanging outside Hardee's. The speech began.

Mubarak's Second Speech

I speak to you during difficult times that have put Egypt and its people to the test; times that seem to be taking it and them to the unknown.

"Get to the point, mister. We don't have time for empty words."

The events of the past days dictate that we, people and leadership, choose between chaos and stability.

"Chaos and stability, again!"

I have taken the initiative of forming a new government with new priorities and a new mandate that would address the demands and aspirations of our youth.

"A new government that brings together all the thieves and criminals!"

I have never been in pursuit of power or fortune . . . . The people know the difficult circumstances under which I shouldered the responsibility . . . and what I have given to the homeland in war and in peace. I am a military man and would never betray what I have been entrusted with nor would I abandon my sense of duty and responsibility.

"Come on, man, get on with it. Don't come begging for pity now."

"Indeed! You've been glued to that chair for thirty years and you want to pass it on to your lovely son."

In all honesty and despite the current circumstances, I had no intention of running for a new presidential term. I have already spent most of my life in the service of Egypt and its people.

"No kidding! So you had no intention of running for another term?"

I want to be clear: I will use the remaining months of my term to ensure a peaceful transition of power within the bounds of my constitutional mandate.

"What are you talking about? You still want to stay on longer?"

"Leave!"

The one word that all the protestors gathered in front of the screen repeated over and over again.

"I call upon .... I demand .... I will oversee .... I will delegate ...."

"Blah blah blah!"

Hosni Mubarak, the man who is addressing you today, is proud of the years he spent in the service of Egypt and its people. This dear country is my home-land, just as it is the homeland of every other Egyptian. I have lived in it and have gone to war for it; I have defended its land, its sovereignty, and its inter-ests. It is on this land that I will die. History will judge me and others, for better or worse.

"Words, words, and more words; that's all you have to offer. What a lame speech. All the appointments that he is now promising he should have made in 2005. Too late, Mr. President!"

Some started to laugh, others looked gloomy and confused, while others still had tears in their eyes. Different arguments began to circulate in the midan: we should go home and give the president a chance to fulfill his promises; we should stay in the midan and continue what we started until the downfall of the whole regime.

"This is enough, guys. Let's let him be for another nine months."

"People, have some mercy. The man wants to die in his own country."

"Let him die. We're not stopping him."

"We can't just leave now."

"Why not? He already said that he would implement changes."

"If we go now, guys, State Security is going to round us all up."

"It's true. They have pictures of us. I see people sticking their cameras in our faces all day long."

"State Security will finish us off, not just round us up. There aren't enough prisons for us all."

"Let's go home, guys, and see what he will do. He may keep his promise."

"People, if we go now, he will avenge himself. You can't be serious."

"The most secure place now is Tahrir."

"No one is to leave, guys."

Some people left while others stayed. We were overcome by a general feeling of doubt, worry, and depression. I left the mattress and the blanket near the tank at the entry point at Talaat Harb Street. One of the young protestors asked me if he could lie down on the mattress for a little while.

"Go ahead. But take good care of it."

Those who remained in the midan gathered in circles, small and large. They discussed the speech and what to do next. There was a rumor that undercover agents and State Security personnel were in the midan. We began to be suspicious of any stranger who stood near us to listen to our conversation. We started an ID check among ourselves.

"Your ID, please."

People willingly showed their ID cards. We would check the occupation: civil servant, teacher, student, and so on. We would apologize to them and show them our own ID cards.

"Here, take a look at my ID card."

"No, it's okay."

"No, it's not okay. We just checked your ID, so you should check ours. We've got to do it right."

We spent most of the night doing this. The euphoria of the million-man march that morning was replaced by suspicion and anxiety.

I went and sat in the midan's central garden with some friends. Some people circulated, continuing to warn other groups: "Be careful, guys. There are undercover agents and State Security people in the midan."

"We already know that. There's nothing we can do about it."

One of the young protestors who was sitting close by started to joke around with a friend of mine. She didn't like it and insisted on checking his ID. There was a blank in the "occupation" space.

"Get out of here quietly."

The young man got up mumbling words we did not care to make out. A man in his fifties and a small child walked by with a loaf of bread and an *al-Ahram* newspaper in hand. He split the loaf of bread in half and showed it to people.

"This is the KFC meal, ladies and gentlemen. And here are the fifty euros."

We smiled and joked with him.

"Can I have a drumstick, please?"

"Here you go," he said, extending a piece of bread.

"Where are the fifty euros, mister?"

"There you go," he replied, ripping off a piece of the official newspaper that had turned into more of a tabloid.

The man and his son went up to almost everyone who was there, spreading good humor among us once again.

"Thank you! You made us laugh. We were really in need of that."

I went to Pierre Sioufi's apartment because I needed to go to the bathroom. Many of my friends, as well as a younger crowd, were all there discussing the speech. The young ones were optimistic, but the older group was really down.

"Come down to the midan, guys. People are beginning to be less uptight and are laughing. They're staying in the midan. Come down and join them."

Obama declared his support for the Egyptian people and called on Hosni Mubarak to effect an immediate, peaceful transition of power.

"Here we go: Obama has sold out Mubarak. It's over, guys."

"We don't need support from the Americans or the Europeans. We can do it on our own. We don't want anyone to intervene."

We went around the midan to spread the call for another million-man march on Friday that would be called "The Friday of Departure." The music was once again blasting in front of KFC. Shadia was singing "Ya habibti ya Masr," and everyone was singing along. Then, the group song, "Bismillah,

Allahu Akbar," I tried to grab a friend by the arm to dance with him, but he laughed and refused. So, I went to join the circle with others to dance and sing. I felt much better as I jumped up and down; I had more confidence in myself and in others as I stamped my feet on the ground. I was happy again and so was everyone else in the midan, both young and old.

I went looking for the mattress I had left beside the tank and the soldiers with whom we had become quite friendly. One of the members of the coordination committee told me that another member was sleeping on it at the entrance to the metro station.

"One minute and I'll wake him up for you."

"No, let him rest. I'm not sleepy yet. I'm just checking on the mattress because it's not mine."

One of the young protestors seemed displeased with the dancing and the singing.

"All this dancing is out of line. This is a revolution not a wedding party!"

"A revolution does not mean depression. It is uplifting to dance and sing. Try it."

"She's absolutely right," said one of the soldiers, joining the conversation.

"And you look like you are on cookies," he added.

"Cookies?"

"Cookies that make you high."

"Please could you try to be polite to me? Being in a revolution does not mean that there are no boundaries. Watch what you say and show respect toward those who are older than you."

"I didn't mean any harm."

"Whatever it is that you mean, let's be respectful toward each other."

I went back to the circle and danced till I was totally exhausted. I wanted to sleep.

I went to Pierre's apartment. All the rooms had already been taken, and so were all the sofas and armchairs. I sat with those who were waiting for the end of the curfew. The discussion revolved around practical matters: how to help people sleep in the midan and decisions around buying blankets and cleaning supplies.

"I will be responsible for the wellness program," I said, laughing.

"We're certain that you will. It's the most important thing."

I was dying to lie down and sleep. I still had one more hour before the metro resumed its service. I took off my coat and put it on the floor. I was cold. I went to the kitchen and made some coffee with milk.

Finally, I dragged my feet to the metro station at Isaaf with Egypt's flag raised high in my hand. Many people were walking along beside me. Some young men were walking in front of us and were saying, "Don't look to your left. Don't look to your left."

I still took a quick peek to the left. At the exit from the 6th of October Bridge there was a sizable group of people who looked like criminals. It was indeed best not to look or make eye contact with them.

In the metro, I sat with the flag in my hand. Some people smiled at us—we were the ones who had just come from Tahrir; others looked at us with disgust and distrust. The sound of an explosion. I jumped out of my seat.

"Don't be scared. It's the sound of the wheels on the rails."

I was relieved.

"I thought it was the sound of bombs," I said.

The citizens' checkpoints were still on the street and in front of people's homes. One of the boys pointed at my flag saying, "Yes, or no?"

"Yes to what? And no to what? We all said 'no.'"

As I continued walking toward the entrance of our building I heard the same question again and again, "Yes, or no?"

The members of the citizens' checkpoint greeted me with smiles and joy: "Finally, he's going to do what we want."

"What we want is different from what you want," I answered, with a broken voice.

"I mean, he's going to amend the constitution and he won't run for elections again."

"And you believe that? Anyway, in a couple of hours he will be gone. The Americans have sold him out."

"We won't allow the Americans to intervene in our affairs. They have nothing to do with us."

I tried to respond, but only inaudible sounds came out of my mouth. I waved my hand and went home. I threw myself on the bed, and slept like a log.

10

10. Wednesday, February 2, The Battle of the Camel

Midday: At Home

The sound of feet shuffling on the floor, noise, voices shouting "yes," incomprehensible sentences. I opened my eyes and shut them again. The sounds returned in less than a few minutes. I slowly opened my eyes and looked around me. I was in my bed. "Yes to Mubarak!" The chant was being repeated aloud but without enthusiasm. I opened the window and peeked out: a rather small group of young people and children marching with large posters of Mubarak. They looked quite suspicious.

I made some coffee and started getting ready to leave.

"Why are you going out again?" my mother asked, visibly disturbed.

I shrugged my shoulders since I found the question rather strange.

"It's over. Mubarak will do what you want and will not run for the upcoming elections."

"Do you believe that nonsense?"

"Enough! Have pity on him. The man wants to die in his country," she said, and she started to cry.

I was shocked to see my mother crying for Mubarak. I laughed despite myself.

"What are you laughing at? You have no feelings. I have been crying all night since his speech."

"Mama, what happened to you? You're crying for Mubarak! What about all those who died? Are you not moved by that?"

"What you are doing is disrespectful. Enough of your insolence! He is an old man. You should all go home and let him finish his term."

"Sure, so that State Security can come and round us up from our homes. Anyway, it is not for me to decide. It is for the people in the midan to decide."

"What people? These kids you've been following around? You should know better than that. I can't believe that you are a university professor!"

"What do you mean by that, Mama? These 'kids' have done what we failed to accomplish when we were their age. And they're not all kids. There are people with us who are around your age in the midan."

She waved her hand at me dismissively and turned on the TV.

Al Jazeera Egypt Channel, breaking news: Violent confrontations in Midan al-Tahrir between demonstrators and riot police personnel in civilian clothes riding horses and camels.

We could see scuffles on the screen. Horses were galloping amid the people and there was a general state of chaos and fear.

"What is this?"

"I don't understand. Wait, let's listen."

Horses galloped into the midan; confrontations between the demonstrators and those riding the horses. It was a very strange scene. Many groups had been trying to access the midan since early morning, but the demonstrators got together and stopped them. They regrouped and started to throw stones and pieces of broken glass. The demonstrators did not retaliate, instead, they kept chanting: "Silmiya! Silmiya!" and "We are brothers!"

The reporter on the television was speaking: "Some of the people in these groups have confessed to us that they have been paid by several businessmen and NDP parliamentarians, like Mohamed Aboul Enein, Ibrahim Kamel, and Hasan Rateb. Some of them confessed that they received between 50 and 100 pounds to stage these counter-demonstrations. But for the moment, the revolutionaries are in firm control of the midan and are practicing self-restraint. But those who try to attack them with weapons are rounded up and handed over to the army."

The anchorwoman interjected, "We will let the images speak for themselves." There were people on camels with swords in their hands making their way into the midan.

"What a disaster! Camels in Midan al-Tahrir? And swords? We're back in the Middle Ages!" I exclaimed.

"Safwat al-Sherif must be behind this," my mother said, as if speaking to herself.

"And you want me to let him stay on until the end of his term? Over our dead bodies."

"Call your sister and find out where she is."

"Her phone is off. I'm leaving now."

"You are not going anywhere," shouted my mother.

"There!" She placed a big chair in front of the door and sat down on it.

"This isn't going to work, Mama."

"Don't go." She defied me with her tears. "Your sister is already out there and we don't know a thing about her."

This was a complicated situation, with my mother and me. I didn't know what to do. We sat down to follow the events on different channels, from different locations in the room: she from the chair positioned in front of the door and I from the sofa. We did not speak. The horses and camels were invading the heart of the midan; swords were being brandished at the demonstrators; the demonstrators were jumping on top of the camels and the horses and dragging down those who were riding them. Confrontations, stone throwing, and many injuries, perhaps even deaths. God protect us! I wanted to go, but I couldn't leave the house. I was going crazy. I wanted to be with the people; I wanted to help; I wanted to do something.

I walked up and down the room. I tried to move my mother from her position. But I failed.

The NDP thugs were on the street chanting, "Yes to Mubarak!" I remembered the march I had seen the day before in Abdeen when they were chanting for Mubarak before his speech. I remembered how divided the midan had become after the speech, the thugs at the exit to the 6th of October Bridge, the mean looks on their faces, and the strange question that morning, "Yes, or No?" I remembered the citizens' checkpoints. To Hell with you, Mubarak! You have divided the people.

My father came back.

"Where's your daughter?" my mother asked him in a terrified voice.

"I don't know. I couldn't get into the midan," replied my father, panting and tired.

"Sit down and rest a bit, Baba, and then tell us what happened."

"I went to Talaat Harb and found that people were throwing stones and running. I heard the sound of bullets. I tried to get to Qasr al-Nil but found that, again, people were throwing stones and empty bottles and running. Some people said to me, 'Go that way. There's a war in the midan.' I told them that my daughter was inside but they said, 'You have to go now. The situation is too dangerous.' I didn't know what to do and her phone is turned off."

"Don't worry, Baba. Her battery must have run out and she's probably busy with what's happening."

"And this one here wants to go too."

"Have pity on us. We can't take this anymore."

"Baba, please let me go."

"Let you go where? I just told you, there's a war out there. Can't you see it on the screen? Camels, horses, and Mubarak's thugs are everywhere on the street."

"Baba, I can't stay. I want to go to the midan."

"You're not going anywhere."

"It's all because you're looking out for yourselves. You're scared that State Security will come and get you. You're scared that you might get sick and not find someone to take you to the hospital. Don't worry, you'll find someone to look after you."

My father grew pale and his features became contracted. I put my hand on my mouth. But what I shouldn't have said was already out.

"I'm sorry, Baba. I really didn't mean it. Baba . . . ."

My father wept.

"No, Baba, I didn't mean it."

I had only seen my father weep once before, when his mother died.

"So how do you like watching your father cry?" said my mother in a tearful voice. She started to cry too.

Oh no, please. No drama.

I held my father and kissed his forehead, then did the same with my mother. I cried despite myself.

"I'm sorry, Baba."

"This is an insult to my patriotism. Do you think I haven't served this country? Shame on you! How can you say that I'm looking out for myself?"

"I swear I didn't mean it."

"Go if you want to. No one will stop you."

I looked at my elderly parents and their shrunken, aging bodies, the wrinkles that had been deepened with anxiety and grief, their contracted bodies in the armchairs, awaiting our return, my sister and I. I wanted to go, but I couldn't leave them like that. I decided I would stay with them for a while and try to make up for some of my rudeness and then leave in the evening.

Midday: Downtown

We were just leaving a friend's house on Huda Shaarawi Street on our way to Tahrir when we saw groups of thugs with sticks on the street. We walked past them toward Qasr al-Nil Street where we saw many people carrying stones and weapons. So we tried Talaat Harb but it was the same scene. We didn't know where to go. We bumped into the guy who runs the Internet café next door to Estoril restaurant. He dragged us inside the shop and bolted the door. We remained inside with a group of foreigners and we could overhear swearing and shooting outside. We tried to call the emergency numbers that the army had announced but there was no answer. They were playing dead. Two hours later, it seemed quieter outside. The owner of the café had hardly unbolted the door when we saw two hands trying to force their way through: one was holding a knife and the other was dripping with blood. These thugs made their way in, forcing us to run up to the second floor. They kept asking the owner who we were and what we were doing in the shop. He told them that we had nothing to do with what was going on and that we had been using the Internet.

The thugs told him that he had to chuck us out. "We want them outside," they said. The owner was negotiating with them and telling them that we lived near the shop and had nothing to do with Tahrir. So they said, "We'll take them home to make sure they don't go to Tahrir." The owner was a wonderful man and he accompanied us back to our friends' house. All along the way, the thugs kept saying, "How can you do this to your country?" That Mohamed ElBaradei has gotten to you. How can you be so brainwashed?" We kept telling them that we had nothing to do with it. They made us feel like we were scum and traitors.

I went to Bab al-Shaariya to buy a small burner, a big pot, and glasses to make ginger for the people in the midan, because ginger is good for your voice and it gives you energy. I had no idea that the thugs were all over the streets—I had not watched any television. In the ginger shop, I innocently said that I was buying these things for the people in Tahrir. People started to give me strange looks and one of the vendors swore at me and said, "Get out of here, girl!" As I was walking on the street, I saw people sitting at coffee shops, asking what these demonstrators were doing and what they wanted. "They take money from foreigners to destroy the economy and the country," they were saying. I stood by to listen. One of them asked me, "What are you standing here for? Give me your ID. I'm going to call the cops. You look like you're one of them, one of the Tahrir people." I ran as quickly as I could.

On another street, I saw people watching TV. I stood with them. Sayyid Ali, the anchor on the Mehwar channel, was hosting a woman who was saying that she had trained in Israel but that she had repented and that the people in Tahrir were traitors and hoped they would come to their senses. I finally understood what was happening. People were against us because they had been telling them we were traitors. I walked away quickly before anyone could notice my presence.

On my way back to Tahrir, one of my girlfriends called me and told me not to come back, "Tahrir is full of shooting, glass, and stone throwing." But I wanted to go back. I wanted to take part and help. I could see that the thugs were on all the streets in Downtown. They really looked like paid thugs, straight out of the slums. Some young men were marching with a badly written sign that said: "The Youth of Duwiqa are Loyal to Mubarak, the Faithful Leader." They were chanting for Mubarak. I was scared of them, but I didn't know what else to do but go back to Tahrir. I got to the tank and stood by it for protection. The thugs also stood by the tank and started to insult the protestors in Tahrir. One of the soldiers said to me, "Get out of here. Don't go to Tahrir." So I held on to his arm and said, "I want to go in. Help me go in."

Midan al-Tahrir: Afternoon

I was standing in the middle of the midan, talking to people and to my friends. The numbers were not very big and people were scattered. One of my girlfriends called me and said, "They're coming to get you on camelback." So I laughed and said, "What camels?" She said, "Now, seriously, there's a lot of camels." I kept on laughing. Then my sister arrived, looking terrified because she had seen them in Mohandiseen near the Mostafa Mahmoud Mosque. They had knives and swords and had surrounded her and her friends and started insulting them. As I stood there, I suddenly saw large groups of people entering the midan on foot from almost all the entry points until they got to Hardee's. They kept swearing at the protestors and started ripping the posters and the signs that we had hung up. Then, in came the camels.

I was standing by the museum. I suddenly saw the camels arriving. I couldn't believe my eyes. And I crossed over to the other side to take photographs of the show. But suddenly, I was face to face with a camel and the guy riding it started brandishing his sword at me. I ran away as fast as I could.

In the beginning, people didn't understand what was happening, but once they did, they started jumping on top of the camels and the horses, forcing their riders off and then arresting them. They searched one of them in front of me and discovered that he was a police sergeant. Then they handed them over to the army and people tied the camels to the tanks that were stationed in Tahrir Street.

The soldier helped me into Tahrir. I saw a shower of stones raining down on people. I saw a friend of mine collecting stones. She said, "Help the demonstrators and start collecting stones." I hesitated for a moment and said, "But we are peaceful demonstrators." She said, "They're killing us." So I started collecting stones in empty boxes of bottled water and in plastic bags. We handed them over from one group to another until the stones reached the frontlines. After a while, a man told us, "The women should stay in the back." So we said, "It's none of your business. We are your equals in this country." Other men also answered him saying, "Yes, they are just like us. Let them help collect the stones." Another man kept insisting that we retreat, "No, they go to the back. We die first." My friend and I started laughing despite ourselves. My friend replied, "We either live together or die together." And we continued collecting stones. The older women and children began pounding the stones against the metal railing, just like drums of war. A man sitting beside us was in the process of making something that we initially couldn't quite discern. We discovered that he was creating strange helmets with empty cardboard boxes and plastic water bottles. He then tied them at ear level with a rope and gave them to people to wear on their heads.

At first, many people were injured because no one really understood what was happening. Then the tanks by the museum and Midan Abdel Moneim Riyad moved a bit to make way for the thugs and the soldiers disappeared inside the tanks. We found ourselves face to face with the thugs. Intuitively, people began organizing themselves. We found ourselves holding each other's hands to create lines and move forward together. Some people were making roadblocks with the railings and the charred parts of the vehicles left in the midan since Friday. Those at the frontlines were throwing stones. When people were injured, they retreated, and others carried them to the makeshift clinic, while others still replaced them. Sometimes even the injured went back after the doctors in the clinic had treated their injuries. All those who were there, whether simple people, ordinary youth, or Ultras, all were saying that this was our final battle and that we had to hold on to the midan. If we withstood the attack, we would prevail.

I came early with two of my friends from Zamalek and we stayed in the midan for a while. Our numbers were less than the million-man march of the day before. Some people were sitting in the garden, kids were playing, others were chatting as they strolled around the midan. We decided to go to see Pierre in his ninth-floor apartment. Many people of different ages were there. Suddenly, we heard a lot of noise. We went to the balcony and saw Mubarak's thugs arriving in great numbers through Talaat Harb and Tahrir streets, and other entry points as well. They were smashing cars on their way. I was nailed to the ground and was petrified. I started to scream. Suddenly, an officer started shooting in the air, so the thugs retreated and began throwing stones from a distance. He shot another two bullets in the air. People started chanting, "The army and the people are one hand," and they got on top of the tanks and started hugging the soldiers and the officer. People then started collecting stones and pressed forward and were able to chase the thugs all the way to Midan Talaat Harb. But they tried to come back. People continued to collect stones to throw at the thugs. These skirmishes went on for a while until the thugs finally went elsewhere. Then people started chanting "The people demand the removal of the regime." We chanted along with them as we stood on the balcony. They attacked again on other streets and on Qasr al-Nil Bridge. Whenever people at the entry points saw groups of thugs, they would pound on the metal railings to alert those inside the midan so that they could get ready. I wanted to go home, but I was too scared to go out. A group of young people went out to help the injured—there were many. Another group was making lentil soup in a huge pot in the kitchen for the people in the midan. Pierre took photos of what was happening and then uploaded them to Facebook when the Internet connection came back.

Mubarak really has gone mad.

Downtown: Evening

I reckoned that the people at the frontlines must be exhausted from confrontations with the thugs and probably needed some food. I wanted to use the bathroom, so I went to Pierre's place. I told those who were there that I was going to Bab al-Louq to buy food and juice. They all chipped in, but I wanted someone to go with me. Some were too scared, others were busy watching what was happening, and others still were too engrossed in conversation. So I went on my own. I was a bit scared on the street, so I asked a man in a gallabiya to accompany me. He came along. The shop owners were a bit startled at the quantities of food and juice that I was buying, and they eyed me with hostility. When the cashier at the supermarket got on the phone, I thought she was reporting me, but then it turned out to be a regular phone call. I was relieved. I divided the bags between me and the man, but on our way back, they wouldn't let us through the checkpoints. They kept saying that the people in Tahrir were paid traitors and did not deserve to be fed. I kept telling them that the food was for the injured on both sides. They finally let us through the first checkpoint. "We'll let you go through for the sake of the injured," they said. I suddenly felt that I had lost my sense of direction, and it was dark too.

At another checkpoint they said, "You won't go through here. Get permission from the checkpoint over there." I could no longer see clearly and the man who was with me had no idea what was going on. We went to the other checkpoint but they wouldn't let us through. So someone said, "Come with me. I'll take you through another route." To tell you the truth, I was scared. The man looked scary. I didn't want to follow him.

I went back to where I had come from. I looked for the man who had come with me, but he had disappeared with the food that he was carrying. I was really angry and tired. They must have confiscated the food he had with him. I couldn't go back to buy more food, nor could I carry more than what I already had. When I was on Tahrir Street, I met some doctors from the makeshift clinic at the mosque on their way to buy medical supplies. They helped me with the bags until we got to the mosque. I distributed the juice and food that I had to the injured in the mosque and nearby.

The Abdel Moneim Riyad and Egyptian Museum Frontlines

The thugs came in consecutive waves. No sooner were we done with one group and were successful in securing the street than they would attack from the other side. People would immediately begin pounding on the metal railings and start smashing stones. This went on all night. The worst was the Abdel Moneim Riyad frontline. Besides the thugs who were throwing stones and Molotov cocktails, there were snipers on the 6th of October Bridge and maybe even on the rooftop of the Ramsis Hilton. The army just turned a blind eye. They hid inside the tanks, and the officers and higher ranks disappeared inside the museum. We continued throwing stones at the thugs. We would advance and throw stones for a while and then retreat to catch our breath. I suddenly saw a friend of mine from the Muslim Brotherhood with a stone in his hand, laughing. He said to me, "So, I want to ask you a question. I'm going to die and go to paradise. How about you? As a leftist, I mean?" I laughed. He said, "So, you really do believe in what we are doing?" I answered him, "Yes, I believe in this country." We laughed together. He was silent for a bit and then he said to me, "My view of things has completely changed because of these events . . . ." Then we went forward and started throwing stones again.

I was distributing water to people with a friend of mine, when suddenly, a young man came up to us and gave us his bag. He said to me, "Here is my bag and my ID is inside it. Please take it to my parents." "Where are you going?" I asked him. He replied, "I am going to my death. I am going to become a martyr." And he ran to the frontline. I was struck dumb. I took the bag and took off to Merit.

Merit

I went to make hot ginger at Merit. Hashem, the owner, looked at me and said, "You've got to be kidding!" So I said, "No, I'm not kidding. People need energy." He said, "People want tea." But I made twenty glasses of ginger and took them to the midan. People did ask me, "Is this tea? Is this tea?" So I went back and made tea. I tried to get past the crowds to the frontlines because they were the most exhausted and the most in need of energy. When the attacks got rough, I would wait for those who were returning to give them tea and go back to make another round. It was very crowded at Merit: some were making sandwiches for the people in the midan, some were helping the injured, while others were discussing what we should do next. We all kept bumping into each other. I continued making rounds of tea to distribute until 3 a.m., and they continued attacking us.

A Friend's House

We said to ourselves that we couldn't go on throwing stones when they were attacking us with bullets and Molotov cocktails. So I took two bottles and got some gasoline and kerosene and told myself that I would experiment. And I did, in fact, do two experiments and I took them to the midan and they worked! We went back to Merit and collected all the empty bottles of wine, beer, and soda and we filled them with gasoline from the cars that were parked on the street. We took them to the midan and we started throwing. People cheered when they saw that we were throwing Molotov cocktails and the Muslim Brotherhood looked at us in amazement. All of our friends who lived in Downtown went home to get empty bottles. We filled them and took off to the Abdel Moneim Riyad frontline. We were at it throughout the night.

Home

The atmosphere at home was charged and tense. My parents and I followed the events on television. I felt paralyzed. I kept moving between the living room where the TV was, my bedroom where the computer and Facebook were, and the balcony that overlooked the miserable marches that were cheering for Mubarak. My sister called to let us know that she was well and warned me not to leave the house. The midan was not safe and the secure entrance points shifted at least every half hour.

I browsed through the video clips and images that had been uploaded to the Internet. I couldn't believe how barbaric the scenes were. I spotted my sister in one of the video clips, carrying a tray with glasses in the middle of the crowds and I saw several friends throwing stones at the enemy, my own compatriots. I recognized some of those who had been injured. I knew them; some of them were with me in the coordination committee and others I used to see in the midan. I was with these people. Simple, beautiful, kind people. I shared the images with my parents. I could see grief in their eyes. I stopped at an image of one of the doctors of the midan embracing one of the soldiers whose eyes were filled with tears.

"I know this soldier! I was talking to him yesterday, I mean early this morning."

My father looked more closely at the image.

"This is not a soldier. He's an officer. He has three stars on his epaulet. Can't you tell the difference between a soldier and an officer?

I was heartbroken. I wanted to be with these people. I wanted to be with the people I had lived with since January 25.

I followed some of the comments of my anti-revolution friends: 'Enough is enough!' was the gist. I was really pissed, so I wrote:

To those who are still defending Mubarak and still want him to finish his term, here is his first reaction: he sent his armed party thugs to kill people. Wake up! The regime is ready to exterminate us all for its own interests. The injured are dying, there are no ambulances, there are no firemen, and no decent police officers. Yes, enough is enough. Step down now if you are really concerned for this country. Enough arrogance! (Facebook, February 2)

I was going crazy. I wanted to go out but was afraid to go alone. I was afraid to take a cab or be with people I didn't know. I was afraid of the citizens' checkpoints that had asked me in the morning if I was for or against. I pleaded with my friends on Facebook who lived in Heliopolis and Nasr City to pick me up and take me with them to Tahrir. I pleaded and waited for an answer from anyone, until I fell asleep in front of the computer.

11
Thursday, February 3

Finally, one of my friends from Heliopolis called to say that he was going to Tahrir. We agreed to meet in Midan Hadayeq al-Qubba and to go to Tahrir via Salah Salem Road and then through Downtown. I put on heavy clothes and a coat; I covered my head with a woolen shawl and put on large sunglasses over my prescription ones. I kissed my father and mother.

"What have you done to yourself?"

"I'm incognito."

My mother laughed and said, "Why don't you find a picture of Mubarak and stick it on your chest."

"Is that a joke or are you being serious? I don't get where you stand anymore."

"Get going, we have things to do."

"Look after yourself and your sister."

"Yes, Baba, but you know my sister: she has a mind of her own. The flag! I was going to forget to take the flag."

I held the flag I had bought in my hand. I wasn't sure whether to take it or not. It had become damning proof of 'No.' I pulled out the plastic pole that supported the flag, folded it, and hid it in my bag. When I got to Tahrir I could hold it.

I left the house and walked against the traffic toward the Qubba Bridge and Roxy. I avoided eye contact with members of the citizens' checkpoint. I didn't want anyone to recognize me. I got to Midan al-Hadayeq and waited for my friend by the bridge as agreed. A man came by with recharge cards for cell phones. I bought several cards and started to recharge my father's phone. I tried to enter the code several times but failed. My friend arrived and I hopped in.

"The cards are all busted. Can you believe that?"

"Where did you buy them?"

"Just now, on the street."

"Nobody buys cards on the street, you know!"

"You're right."

I noticed his left hand. It was bandaged.

"What happened?"

"A stone from yesterday's battle."

"Were you in the midan yesterday?"

"Of course, where else would I be? It was a battle for real and people were very heroic. They were very determined, despite the number of injured. Morale was very high and we all encouraged each other. People fought over who would be on the frontlines: I will die first. No, I will die first."

"Incredible. I really wanted to be with you. I was going crazy being stuck at home."

"It was dangerous to get there. We were unable to tell people which route to take. The thugs were attacking at very short intervals. And the attacks continued until this morning near Abdel Moneim Riyad."

"Until now? What about the army?"

"Like thin air—as if they were not there!"

We stopped at a checkpoint to have the car searched and the license checked. One of the young men cleared us, tapped on the car, and we drove through.

"I don't know why I can't stand these citizens' checkpoints. They screwed us last night in Downtown. They confiscated food, drinks, and medical supplies that were coming to Tahrir."

"I don't know how you survived yesterday."

"Yeah, it was very difficult. But we actually didn't have time to think. We had to act quickly, each as he saw fit. The strange thing is that when people saw the thugs coming toward us in groups, they quickly stood together and locked their arms as if they had been trained to do so. They attacked them and fought with their bare hands and feet. Then came the stone throwing, Molotov cocktails, metal rods, and swords! But we were able to stand up to them. The nice thing is that people also helped the thugs who were injured and carried them to the makeshift clinics and the doctors treated both sides. They were stretched out side by side with the protestors—just like that. You know what? We are a very kind people."

We parked the car on a side street, off Emad al-Din Street, far enough from any potential attack. We walked to Midan Talaat Harb. The shops were open and people were walking quite normally, just like us, as if there had not been a war in the midan until that very morning! The checkpoints started immediately after Midan Talaat Harb. My friend went to the men's queue and I went to the one for women. The "No Parking" sign by the sidewalk had a piece of paper stuck on it that read, "Leave, Mubarak." The word "leave" was underlined twice in red. People started to come back to the midan. It seemed like the Battle of the Camel had brought about a reversed outcome: instead of dispersing the protestors, their numbers increased. How stupid you are, Hosni Mubarak! You and all those who advise you!

What I had watched on the television screen was one thing and what I was witnessing at the moment was another. I couldn't believe the number of injuries. It seemed like everyone had been hurt: in the head, the arm, the leg, the foot, or the eye, and many had multiple injuries. The sheer amount of stones that were thrown in the midan and on the streets! I couldn't believe that the midan that I had left clean, organized, and bustling with signs and posters of our demands after the million-man march on Tuesday had come to this. The posters and the sketches by the Revolutionary Artists' Alliance had been torn down and some of the big loudspeakers had been smashed. I walked among the people as if in a daze. All I could say was, "Thank God you're well," and "May you get better soon." Despite the injuries and the visible pain on people's faces, they were still smiling at each other. They were even telling jokes:

"Mubarak challenges boredom!"

"With Mubarak, you are always on your toes."

Their eyes were full of determination and resolution to stay in the midan until Mubarak stepped down. An Egyptian friend of Armenian origin called to tell me that he was going to Tahrir. I told him that I was already there. He asked me if we needed anything, so I told him that I would ask the doctors and call him back. I walked toward the closest makeshift clinic, the one that had been set up inside a shop that was still under construction at the beginning of Qasr al-Nil Street. A doctor was extracting something from the forehead of someone lying on a large table. A female doctor was changing the bandage on the arm of another injured person. I saw someone who had been hurt in the leg, the head, and the arm but was using his other arm to write on the wall: "We are not tired, we are not tired. This is the price of freedom." Despite the general horror of the scene, I was smiling. These simple people were real heroes. When she had finished, I asked the doctor to give me a list of the medical supplies that were needed. I called my friend and dictated it to him.

Huge numbers arrived in the midan. Suddenly the chanting rose:

"The people demand the removal of the president!"

The masses in the midan chanted along. The chant had changed from "The people demand the removal of the regime," to "the people demand the removal of the president." The people don't want you, Mubarak! Don't you understand? You divided the people with your miserable, pathetic speech. You brought back the people to the midan with your own stupidity.

"Leave!"

"Leave means go! In case you didn't know!"

"Speak to him in Hebrew! He doesn't understand Arabic!"

The people of the midan used all languages and dialects to try to make Mubarak understand. One young man held a sign, with an airplane underneath, that read: "Your final airstrike will be in Saudi Arabia," in a sarcastic reference to the first airstrike during the 6th of October War that Mubarak had trumpeted for the past thirty years, as if he had been the only pilot. It was also a reference to the fact that Saudi Arabia would give him asylum, like the runaway Tunisian Ben Ali. People gathered around the young man and started commenting on his sign.

"Saudi Arabia probably doesn't want him. One dictator is enough for them."

"And they say that torrential rains have submerged Saudi since they took Zein al-Abedin. God's vengeance!"

"Saudi Arabia doesn't want to take him for fear that they would have a revolution too."

"It doesn't have to be Saudi Arabia, guys. He can go to Germany. Didn't he go for treatment in Germany?"

"Or Italy. Isn't he good friends with Berlusconi?"

"Or to Israel, his big buddy."

"What would they do with him? It's over now."

"The US?"

"Obama has already ditched him. He told him to step down now."

"So where will he go?"

"He can go to Hell. It's not our problem. He's the one who did this to us and to himself."

I continued walking around the midan. I saw some of the loot from the Battle of the Camel suspended from traffic lights: a horseshoe, a saddle, a whip, and a decorated camel harness. There were also informational signs: "The Battle of the Camel took Place Here." I didn't know whether I should laugh or cry about this farce. Then, the campaign to clean and organize the midan began. There were different working groups: some swept the ground, some collected the stones, and some collected the garbage and carried it to the edges of the midan. I helped sweeping with some friends. Children and young demonstrators took the rocks and created installations on the ground. There was a big painting of an airplane with Mubarak's face in the middle crossed out. The text below the drawing read: "Fly Away Now." What a people! Beautiful and civilized! Even the stones were used in artistic ways. We had been so tainted by this regime that brought out the worst in us.

I passed by Merit to make sure that my friends were all right; then, I called the friend who said he would bring the medical supplies.

"Where are you, man?"

"I sent the stuff with friends from Zamalek and I double-checked that they made it into Tahrir."

"And why didn't you come? Didn't you say you were coming?"

"I did come with two of my workers at the factory. We tried to go through the Downtown entry to the midan. We tried to get the stuff in, but that stupid citizens' checkpoint wouldn't let us in and they wanted to confiscate the supplies. So we went round and tried Zamalek. I tried to enter from Qasr al-Nil Bridge but they wouldn't let me through. They said I was a foreigner."

"A foreigner?" I laughed, "Of course, you're blond and you have blue eyes."

"I kept telling them, 'I'm Egyptian,' and my workers did too, but it was hopeless. They said 'Show us your ID card,' so I showed it to them. 'There! It says Egyptian.'"

"And of course they couldn't read your name."

"They said, 'You're a spy,' and they kept pounding on the car and saying, 'Get out of here.'"

"I told them, 'How can I be a spy? I've done my military service!' But there was no way they were going to let me through. So stupid."

"It's okay. It's just that your name . . . . I mean, is there anyone in the world with a name like that with 'Artin' and 'yan' at the very end? How will you meet your Maker with a name like that?"

"Beats me."

"Here, we are called either Mohamed or Girgis. Change your name, man, and avoid this headache!"

"It's okay. The important thing is that the stuff got there."

"Glad you're well, my dear, and thanks for your help."

I went back to the midan entry point at Talaat Harb to say hello to my colleagues and comrades in the coordination committee. They had all been injured but nevertheless were steadfast in their position.

"Unbelievable," I murmured to myself.

The mattress I had borrowed from my friend had been thrown beside the stones and the garbage. It had turned black and was covered with stains. It was no good anymore. One of my colleagues saw me.

"Sorry about the mattress."

"Don't worry about it. The most important thing is that you are well. I'm actually surprised that it is still here after the battle."

I greeted the soldiers I knew. Many were greeting and embracing the officer I had mistaken for a conscript. I walked toward him with my arms wide open.

"May I hug you and kiss you?"

"No, no, no, no!"

I laughed at how shocked he was and I shook his hand with both my own.

"I am very proud of you."

"Thank you."

"I saw your photo on Facebook last night and I wrote that I knew you. I'm sorry I said you were a soldier. I didn't know that you were an officer."

"That's okay. Don't worry about it."

Someone called him: "Captain Maged Boulos?"

He embraced him.

"Is your name Maged Boulos?"

"Yes, but I go by Maged Gamal."

"Excuse me, I really don't like to speak about people in terms of whether they are Muslim and Christian, but I will write on Facebook that the Egyptian officer Maged Boulos opened fire on the thugs and defended the protestors in Tahrir so that people will understand that there is no difference between us."

The memory of the bombing of the Church in Alexandria earlier that month was still vivid in my mind and that of many Egyptians, especially the Christians.

Captain Maged smiled, "No need to do that."

"No, it's important. People have to know and understand."

"Okay. Write whatever you want."

And so I went up to Pierre's apartment and asked to use the computer. I shared Captain Maged's photo and wrote my comment.

The call for the "Friday of Departure" began to circulate on Facebook and in the midan. With nightfall, the number of people increased. Many finished work and came in groups to Tahrir. Some brought sandwiches, kushari, water, and juice for those who had been sitting in. As the call spread, the number of tents increased and many decided to spend the night in Tahrir. During the night, several groups appeared with new blankets and started to distribute them to those who needed them. New big loudspeakers were brought to the midan to replace those that had been destroyed and the radio service resumed with different songs, speeches, and poetry. In addition, TV screens were tuned to Al Jazeera. People began to sit on the ground and what remained of the empty spaces in the gardens surrounding the midan. Some groups were engaged in conversation, other groups were singing, some had lit fires and were making tea. I joined a group that was singing patriotic songs. I sang along with them: "Ya habibti ya Masr," "Ya aghla ism fi-l-wugud," "Helwa baladi al-samra." We were intoxicated with joy and happiness. Then, one man began to sing the lyrics of "Khalli al-silah sahi"—keep your weapon awake. Yes, right! We have to be careful, guys.

"Keep your weapon awake and by your side.

If the whole world sleeps, I will remain awake with my weapon by my side

My weapon in hand by day and by night,

Calling to the rebels: treachery fills our enemy.

Keep your weapon awake and by your side."

My eyes filled with tears as I chanted in my broken voice, "Awake, awake." It was very painful to think that the enemy was of us, from among us, of our people and from our family. What weapon did we have in our hands? Stones and rocks? And why? We didn't want to kill each other.

Most of the people expected Mubarak to step down the next day.

"Yes, but he still has one more speech to go, like Ben Ali."

"Yes, you're right. He still hasn't said, 'Now I understand you, I understand you.'"

"But what can he say now, after what he did yesterday? Would he have the nerve to speak?"

I spent the evening strolling in the midan. I did my rounds, standing with the members of the organization and search committees. We sang and encouraged each other and waited for tomorrow: the day of departure, the departure of Mubarak.

12

February 4,
Friday of Departure

One of the people who had been sleeping on the floor got up. I immediately took his place. I was dying to sleep for a couple of hours. I quickly fell asleep and dreamed that I was twenty years old and had just finished my PhD thesis and was waiting for my defense. The defense was postponed, but I wasn't upset, nor were the young men and women who surrounded me. Instead, we exchanged jokes and gags. What mattered was that I had finished the thesis; the defense could be whenever. We ate roumi cheese sandwiches together. I opened my eyes and looked around me. I was on the floor in Pierre's apartment. I looked at the clock on the wall; it was 6:30 a.m. I had barely slept for half an hour. Mubarak will not step down today. I went to the balcony and looked out onto the midan. Some people were jogging around the central garden; others were preparing breakfast and tea. The radio station that had been recently set up in front of Hardee's was broadcasting the latest news and was listing the assets and property of prominent figures in the regime, starting with Mubarak and his sons. Some people were still sleeping inside and around the midan, in front of stores and the entrances to apartment buildings. I recounted my dream to the first person who came to the balcony. He looked out onto the midan and made no comment. He went to the kitchen to make coffee and then came back to the balcony with two cups.

"But you were not upset in the dream?" he asked.

"No, not at all. I may have been a bit upset, but later in the dream, I was joking with my friends."

"This means that this long-winded showdown will go on."

We smiled at each other—the first smile of the morning. A long-winded showdown indeed.

I washed my face and went out to the midan. I bid good morning to my comrades, the soldiers, and the officers. Dalida was singing "Helwa ya baladi" on the radio station at Hardee's. One of my friends grabbed my arm and we danced together and sang along with Dalida:

> A pretty song or two.
> You are beautiful, my dear country.
> My hope has always been
> To return to you, my country,
> And to remain forever by your side.
> My heart is filled with stories.
> Remember them, my country?
> My first love was in my country.
> How can I ever forget?
> We used to say that parting is impossible.
> Nothing is sweeter than the words "my country"
> In a song or in a refrain.
> *Ya leil ya ein.*

People gathered around us, and some joined the dancing and singing while others clapped their hands. Some fully veiled women swayed the flags in their hands to the rhythm of the music. We laughed and looked around us: smiling, happy, hopeful faces. The song ended, but its invigorating and heartwarming effect remained.

"Have you had breakfast?"

"No."

"Let's get some sandwiches and go to the coffee shop."

"You go. I can't walk. I only slept for twenty minutes. I'll wait here for you."

My friend took off to Bab al-Louq, and I sat at the coffee shop on Tahrir Street, facing two tanks and soldiers who were still wiping away traces of sleep from their faces and clothes.

"Fuul and taamiya! So where are the KFC meals that they are distributing?"

We devoured the sandwiches with joy and then had black coffee.

"Let's go for a walk in the midan."

"Yes, let's."

I grabbed my friend's arm and we strolled through the midan and chanted together, "We used to say that parting is impossible."

And we laughed!

"No, it's not impossible, Mubarak!"

We lingered by humorous signs that were at once funny and innovative:

"Leave, My Arm Is Aching."

"Leave, My Wife Wants to Give Birth."

"ctrl+alt+delete-Mubarak."

It made me think of the sign I had made earlier: "Now I Can Get Married and Have Children. There is Hope in the Future." But I couldn't remember where I had left it. I thought to myself: so what is it that I want now? To be honest, what I wanted was a shower.

I left my friend in the midan and went up to Pierre's apartment. I took a white sheet of paper and wrote: "Leave, I Want to Shower," and I went back to the midan. I walked around with my sign among my friends and comrades. They all laughed. The soldiers and the officers saw it and they started shouting:

"We want to shower too!"

"So, why don't you tell him? He's your commander-in-chief, isn't he?"

I strolled around the midan with my new sign in hand. Many people took my photo. I found it funny.

Some added, "We also want to shave."

But some of the bearded men looked at me disapprovingly. I shrugged my shoulders. To shower is a human right for all.

The midan and the surrounding streets began to fill up in preparation for Friday prayer. The day before, the Mufti of the Republic had issued a religious decree allowing Friday prayer outside mosques if individuals feared that their lives may be threatened. Ha! After January 28, people were no longer afraid of anything at all, my dear Mufti! For the Prophet's sake, keep your decrees to yourself. People in all the governorates will participate in the demonstrations. The advisor to the Sheikh of al-Azhar had resigned in order not to implicate al-Azhar and had joined people in Tahrir. I walked away from the crowds in order not to get stuck as they prepared for prayer. I went back to the entry point at Talaat Harb Street and joined the organization committee. I noticed the crosses tattooed on many hands that had been locked together in a human chain behind the Muslims who were praying. As soon as the imam ended the prayer, the crowds started chanting:

"The people demand the removal of the regime! The people demand the removal of the president!"

The imam asked the crowds to perform an additional prayer for the souls of the martyrs. The chanting rocked the midan:

"The people demand the removal of the regime!"

I shuddered at the power of the chant as it rose into the air and I secretly prayed to God. He knew what I wanted.

I turned toward an army officer who was talking to the citizens. I didn't quite understand why so many of the high-ranking officers in the midan had such big bellies. Weren't they supposed to exercise? I overheard the officer say,

"The people of Egypt have always been a great people."

I couldn't help interrupting the conversation:

"Excuse me, but before January 25, this same people were filthy, unruly, and outright rude."

"I will not allow you to speak like that about the great Egyptian people," the lieutenant said sharply.

"I'm sorry, but this is the truth. To begin with, you officers don't deal with the people. You have your cars and your buses, your flats and clubs, your supermarkets, your gas stations. Try to walk on the street and you'll see for yourself."

"Still, I will not allow you to speak like that about the great Egyptian people."

"Don't be upset, sir. I'm speaking about the people before January 25. I joined the demonstrations on January 25 and discovered that it was the regime that had tainted us and brought out the worst in us. On January 25, I discovered that we can be a great, civilized, and respectable people."

I couldn't help laughing. There was no prospect for dialogue. It was like talking to a broken record; he kept repeating the same sentence. I ignored him and started chanting with the people.

Suddenly, we heard music—the sound of the duff and the mizmar approaching from behind us. We all turned around. The Upper Egyptians had arrived! We were delighted and we started to laugh and cheer. A big group of Upper Egyptians, young and old, in their distinctive, flowing, dark gallabiyas, with their turbans and woolen kashmir shawls, had arrived at the ID checkpoint. They pulled out their IDs and raised their arms in preparation for the body search. Everyone greeted them and many joined them. They played the duff and the mizmar and people clapped to the rhythm. What a very Egyptian scene. The presence of this group of Upper Egyptians really made a difference. They looked beautiful. So very Egyptian. Especially in their gallabiyas that were different from the Saudi and Gulf region's transparent white ones. Everyone took pictures of the group, even the officers and the soldiers. The midan was overflowing with happiness and joy.

A long yellow banner was then suspended from Pierre's apartment. It was as long as the entire building and carried the demands of the midan: the removal of the president, dissolving the fraudulent upper and lower parliaments, immediate end to emergency law, installing a transitional national unity government, an elected parliament that would amend the constitution in order to hold presidential elections, immediate trials for those implicated in the deaths of the martyrs of the revolution, immediate trials for corrupt officials who had been robbing the country blind. The people in the midan cheered and the flags fluttered. Those on Pierre's balcony chanted with those in the midan:

"The people demand the removal of the regime!"

Thousands continued to flock to the midan from all directions, arriving from different governorates, with Suez in the lead. Both sides of the 6th of October Bridge near the Tahrir exit were transformed into parking lots, as was Qasr al-Nil Bridge and all the streets that led into Tahrir. The Ultras arrived with their drums and flags chanting,

"Raise your head up high, you are an Egyptian!"

Pride and dignity marked the faces of Egyptians, having disappeared for many years. Long live Egypt!

"The president is gone! The president is gone!" I overheard the news circulating among people as they embraced and kissed each other. "The president is gone!"

"Is the president really gone?" I asked someone coming toward me.

"Yes!" he cried ecstatically.

I laughed. Congratulations! Congratulations to all Egyptians. I embraced members of a family who stood beside me. Everyone was doing the same, even though we did not know each other. People got on their cell phones to spread the news.

Then we heard that it was just a rumor.

"Boo!"

"Don't get upset, guys. We all know he won't give in that easily."

"We have to persist. We have to have patience. The most important thing is that we remain in the midan."

The Ultras immediately began chanting their slogans and young and old joined them enthusiastically:

"He must leave! We won't leave!"

"Leave means go! In case you didn't know!"

Once more, the midan was filled with the sound of chants, drums, songs, and a call for more demonstrations on Sunday, Tuesday, and Friday, declaring it the Week of Perseverance.

13
The Week of Perseverance

1

Okay, I really must shower now.

I went to my friend who lives on Champollion Street. The citizens' checkpoint members stopped me at the entrance to the street to check my ID and let me through. I went straight to the bathroom. Oh my God! Hot water! A shower!

I borrowed clothes from my friend and washed my own and hung them out to dry. I covered my head with a wool-embroidered shawl so as not to catch cold, and then I left. I was stopped again by the citizens' checkpoint.

"Where are you going?"

"I'm going to the midan," I answered in surprise.

"No one is allowed into the midan."

"What's going on? I've just come through here."

"This street belongs to us. We own the shops on this street and we will not allow anyone into the midan."

Another person tried to go through; he tried to argue with them.

"We are in deep shit because of you. Nobody comes to the street to get their cars fixed anymore."

One of them turned around and faced me.

"Do you have money?"

"No, I don't."

I really didn't have any money on me, since I had left my handbag at Pierre's and had only taken my ID and cell phone.

Another person asked me, "Are you from Pakistan or Iran, or are you with Hizbollah?"

"What are you talking about? Hizbollah or Pakistan! I'm Egyptian, and here's my ID."

He suspiciously scrutinized my ID card.

"You still won't go through."

I took my ID card and headed for the narrow alleyway of Takaiba coffee shop, then walked around to Mahmoud Bassiouni Street and on to Talaat Harb to the checkpoints that allowed people into the midan. I told my friends about what happened with the checkpoint on Champollion Street.

They laughed and said, "They're right to think that you are Pakistani or Iranian. But you're much fairer after the shower you just took!"

"Haha, not funny!"

"And that shawl on your head makes you look like Benazir Bhutto."

"Even without the shawl, they take me for a foreigner. What can I do?"

Three foreigners in their fifties with bouquets of flowers were walking among the people repeating one word: "Freedom." People welcomed them and smiled back at them. They marched among people from all walks of life and did not fear for their lives.

I asked one of them, "Where are you from?"

"The United States of America."

I immediately remembered the white van with diplomatic plates that had run over the protesters on Qasr al-Aini Street on the Friday of Rage. I also remembered the messages I had received from my American friends, expressing their regret at the catastrophe. These Americans must feel ashamed at the sheer possibility that their embassy was implicated in the killings, even though the Egyptian authorities did nothing to investigate the identity of the murderous driver.

I went back to the organization committee at the entrance to Talaat Harb Street. I stood near a young man named Emad who had been injured in the head, jaw, and arm.

"I'm so sorry! I hope you get well soon."

"Thank you!" he said, laughing.

"Did this happen during the Battle of the Camel?"

"My head and my jaw injuries were caused by birdshot on January 28. I was injured in the arm during the Battle of the Camel."

"Were you on Qasr al-Aini Street on the Friday of Rage?"

"My brother and I were there. He was martyred there."

I felt my entire being collapse and heaviness filled my heart. I looked at the young man and said nothing.

He continued:

"I came with my friends from Bulaq al-Dakrour and we walked to Qasr al-Aini Street. Suddenly, a speeding white van drove into the people and crushed them. As we were picking up the dead bodies and the remains of body limbs, I looked at one of the faces and realized it was my brother. I put his body aside, and I continued picking up the other bodies. I had no time to weep for my brother."

I embraced the young man and kissed his forehead and prayed that his brother, and all those who had died, would rest in peace. Every time Egyptian or foreign journalists or photographers walked past us, I would introduce them to Emad who had become like a young brother to me. He was the only one who was allowed to address me by my name without any title: sister, miss, doctor, professor, madam. Emad was sixteen years old; his brother died on Qasr al-Aini Street. He was twenty. How many more young men like Emad existed in Egypt?

Two of my friends from the organization committee came toward us laughing. One of them was watching something on his cell phone and the other was slapping his hands together in disbelief.

"What's up, guys. Share the joke."

"A high-ranking army officer, a general it seems, whose name is Hasan wanted us to leave the midan and was saying that what we're doing amounted to nothing more than a bad soap opera."

"No kidding!"

"I swear to God. Take a look for yourself. Here, watch the video clip I recorded."

He rewound the clip and we gathered around to watch it:

People were chanting, "The army and the people are one hand." The sound was not very clear. It sounded like the general wanted to remove the makeshift clinic or change its location. The doctor responded, "If you remove the clinic and the army isn't offering any services, then what?" The general didn't answer. A military police officer nearby listened with disgust. One of the young men said, "Make way, come and walk among the people and see the situation with your own eyes." The general said, "I don't need an escort. I am the one who is protecting you." A bearded sheikh responded, "Allah is the sole protector." The general reacted by citing the Qur'anic verse: *And whosoever keepeth his duty to Allah, Allah will appoint a way out for him.* People were still chanting, "The army and the people are one hand." The general said that everything was now being delivered to the midan by helicopter, because all of the military vehicles had been set on fire. He said. "Do you want to know who set them on fire?" The young man replied, "No I don't want to know. I'm not asking." The general said that a gas cylinder cost fifty pounds. There was a shot of an overturned, charred vehicle at Abdel Moneim Riyad Square. A protestor was standing on top of it. The general addressed the young man angrily, "Who do you think you are?" The young man replied, "I am an Egyptian citizen." The general started shouting, "Do you know how much the vehicle you just set on fire costs?" The young man replied, "We didn't set it on fire."

"Has this guy not heard of the Battle of the Camel and the thugs who attacked the midan all day on Wednesday and then again the next day?" "Just watch the rest of the video clip."

A number of military police were removing the roadblocks so that the general could come through. One of the demonstrators said, "Remove the roadblocks, guys." Another explained, "We are being attacked with Molotov cocktails. The thugs threw Molotov cocktails at us. We were butchered on Wednesday." The military police soldiers were pushing back the people. The general was getting upset. He started addressing a woman, "I will be cruel. Do you understand?" The woman answered him, "Yes, I understand. It can't get any worse." She pleaded with him, "Protect them." The general was provoked, "Protect them from what?" She responded, "From the thugs." The general said, "But here you are safe!" She responded, "How about the three hundred people who died?" The general continued, "Yesterday people were asking for our help because they couldn't go home." The woman replied, "And I swear to you that I was here taking photos till three in the morning." He replied, "Where were you exactly?" She continued, "I was all over the midan last night and no one stopped me from entering or leaving. I am an eyewitness." The general moved away from the woman, toward an old man and asked him, "So, what do you want?" The old man replied, "I want Mubarak to go." The general replied, "You should go home. You can't just sit here." The man replied, "I will go after he goes." The general replied, "Okay, stay then, but think of your family and how you'll get paid if you don't go to work."

The general continued walking in the rubble. The young woman said, "Can't you see the stones? The protestors were attacked with these stones. They were peaceful until they were attacked by the thugs." The general replied, "Listen, all this staged drama is meant to put pressure on the government, but no one can pressure the government. This is an independent government that will form an independent government."

"Did you hear that? 'An independent government that will form an independent government.' What does that mean?"

"What is he talking about!"

"Watch this video clip too. In this one, he says that no one died and the doctors in the midan respond to that. The general's only concern is to open the streets and get the traffic going on the bridge."

"I can't believe that his only concern is the streets and the bridge! What about the people who died?"

"Didn't you hear him say it was all staged?"

"So, is the army with us or against us?"

"I don't know."

And I really didn't know. What I did know was that the officers stationed at the entrance to Tahrir near the Egyptian Museum made way for the thugs to come through. I also knew that Captain Maged Boulos opened fire on the thugs here, at the entrance to Talaat Harb. Since then, he had been worried about punitive measures against him, because he opened fire without permission. I also remembered the officers at the TV Building in Maspero who were telling people that they should leave and come back the next day. I really wasn't sure, but I thought we should not make an enemy of the army. Since the appearance of the army on the street, we had bonded: we played soccer together, we ate together, we slept side by side—even when they slept inside their tanks and us outside.

The day went by with its fears and anxieties. In the evening, some young women began making a huge pot of lentil soup, which smelled incredible. I wanted some, but the girl in charge of preparing it refused.

"This is for the people in the midan."

"I am from the midan."

"No. Eat anything else in the fridge."

"Can I just taste it?"

She gave me less than a quarter of a cup. It was fantastic: lentil soup with potatoes, carrots, garlic, and herbs. Two young men carried away the pot, along with cups and a ladle. We started distributing the soup in the midan.

I moved around the midan. I stopped and chatted with members of the organization committee. Then, I went up to Pierre's apartment, then to Merit to use the toilet, quickly get the latest news, and see my friends. We heard reports that a committee of elders had been formed to negotiate with the government and with Vice President Omar Suleiman. Some of the members of the committee were leading figures in the Muslim Brotherhood. The radio station at Hardee's announced that the Sunday sermon would take place in the midan the next day. There would be two sermons: one at 11 a.m. and one at 1 p.m., followed by prayers for Egypt.

While I was standing with the members of the organization committee, some friends came by and took me with them to the midan's central garden to listen to a group of men from Upper Egypt singing "Dhahaba al-laylu wa talaa al-fagru," a popular childhood song by Mohamed Fawzi, but they had changed the lyrics.

"You won't believe your ears. Really creative!"

"I don't know if they've just improvised it or if they had prepared it beforehand. But it's truly fantastic."

We got to the group in the central garden where a big group of people had gathered and were clapping, laughing, and cheering.

"Encore! Again!"
So they sang it again:

Once upon a time in our village,
We had a cocky president.
Cocky.
He thought he owned it all and always he lived the part.
Always lived the part.
So they told him you better stop; this will not work big man.
Big man.
So, he got the soldiers and his thugs and a thousand guards.
A thousand guards.
They stole my country and the bread of my children, young and old.
Young and old.
The whole village said to him, "Stop being such an asshole."
Such an asshole.
The whole village rose against the sons of bitches.
The sons of bitches.
And against the heartless Hosni Mubarak.
The heartless.
The whole village told him, "No, to stop right there!"
Stop right there!
He tried to scare us and terrify us.
So we responded, "Hahaha!"
Hahaha!
You cannot defeat us, because you are thick-skinned.
Skin so thick.
Tomorrow you will melt under the sun of revolution, you statue of wax.
Statue of wax.
Together my son, hand in hand, a step toward change.
Toward change.
To save our beloved country from an evil man.
An evil man.
Let's go, Haridi and Gaidi, hand in hand.
Hand in hand.
We'll bring back your days of glory once again.

Once again.
Soon happiness will fill your lands from north to south.
North to south.
Mother of the world, my dearest one, a new dawn is rising.
And such a new dawn.
True, oh mother of the world, oh dear Egypt, a new dawn is rising.
A new dawn will rise.

2

I did not want to miss the morning sermon, so I tossed and turned as I lay on the floor, looking at the clock on the wall almost every quarter of an hour. Despite the fatigue and the lack of sleep I sprung up as soon as I heard the radio station at Hardee's announce that the sermon was about to begin. I quickly washed my face and left. I was stopped by an army officer I did not know who asked questions about some of the regulars in the midan. Then he asked for my ID. He looked at it and put it in his pocket. I was both surprised and angry.

"Anything wrong, sir? Is there a problem?"

"No, we're just interrogating some people, so we will keep your ID with us for a while."

I felt like someone had just confiscated my driver's license on the road. But I didn't want to begin my day with a fight. So I left my ID with the officer and went to the sermon that was being held in front of Hardee's.

The pastor of the Evangelical Church asked those present to pray for Egypt. Even though the Christian presence was rather small, many Muslims joined in the prayer and the hymns. I felt that we were all one. I believe it was a collective and not an individual feeling.

No matter how dark the Earth,
The sky is full of light.
We are all praying,
O Jesus, bless my homeland,
Bless my homeland,
Bless my homeland.

Everyone chanted "Bless my homeland" from the depths of their hearts. Amen. There was a feeling of love and purity that reigned over the midan. The priest announced that there would be another sermon at 1 p.m. and invited us all to pray once more.

I went to a coffee shop with a friend on a side street off Mohamed Mahmoud. We ordered coffee and sat outside at a table on the sidewalk to keep warm in the sun. I took off my shoes and socks and put my feet up in the sun. I should change my socks. I spotted the officer who had taken my ID standing in front of one of the tanks on the street. He saw me and signaled that I should go to him.

I put on my shoes and walked toward him. He handed me the ID.

"Our apologies, Professor."

"Thank you!"

I went back to the crowded coffee shop and waited for the coffee with my friend. I was falling asleep. I drank my coffee quickly and went back to Pierre's apartment to sleep, even if for just half an hour. A group of young men and women were watching something and laughing.

"What are you laughing at?"

"Come, come!"

A video clip of Mubarak giving one of his previous speeches.

"So, what's so funny?"

"Just listen."

In the Name of God, the Beneficent and the Merciful: Citizens of Egypt. As president of the republic I have repeatedly stressed and will continue to stress my right to practice corruption . . .

I laughed, "What is this?"

"Wait, there's more."

. . . and my right to rob public property and to incite violence and destruction . . .

"This really is incredible!!"

. . . as well as to foster unemployment and poverty. I work toward fulfilling these goals every day of my life. I have never forsaken these commitments. I am firm and unwavering in my pledge to bring about more fires, and to continue to destroy education and health services in order to further destabilize the country and usurp legitimacy. I have asked the government for more violence, chaos, destruction, and ruin. Once more, I repeat that I will be firm

about all necessary decisions to ensure more fear, unemployment, and general setbacks. This is the responsibility I have been sworn to as president. May God protect you all.

"Hilarious! Who's the brains behind this?"

"I don't know, but it's circulating on YouTube. They called it 'Mubarak's Real Speech.'"

"And they used the same background and the logo of the Egyptian TV channel as well as the news headlines at the bottom of the screen. It's very well done."

It's good to fall asleep laughing, but I did not have the time to do that. On my way to the last room in the apartment, a group of friends stopped me.

"Did you read this?"

"Read what?"

"BBC Arabic just had a report on how the army has been torturing demonstrators."

I was astounded. Torture? The army?

I started reading about it. Different correspondents had published testimonies by demonstrators who had been detained and tortured by army personnel inside the Egyptian Museum. There was an image of the officer who had confiscated my ID card that morning dragging a man by the arm. His face was contorted. I could not believe what I was reading, nor did I want to believe it.

"Is this really happening?"

"Yes, it's true," said one of my friends, whose own friends had been subjected to torture. There was no room for doubt. I believed her because I knew her well. She was not lying or making this up. I was confused. I had not experienced anything unpleasant from the officers who were on Talaat Harb Street. But perhaps those who were near the museum were different. The Battle of the Camel had taken place before their very eyes and they did not intervene. Instead, they may have helped the thugs in some way. I thought I would print the report and show it to the officers I knew: Maged Boulos and others. But a friend advised me not to.

"They must have people who are archiving these reports. You stay out of it."

I was tired, and felt down and anxious. I went to the very last room in the apartment and thanked God that it was empty. I lay down on the couch and covered myself with the blankets that were scattered on it. I hid my head. I did not want to think about anything at all. I wanted to sleep. I just wanted to sleep. But the sounds from the midan and those of the sermon, as well as the voices of friends, all reached me and my desire for sleep disappeared, even though I desperately needed to rest. I went out on the balcony and looked out at the midan. It was joyful. Preparations were underway for a concert. I guess that was exactly what I needed: a party.

I tried to move closer to the stage but failed because of the thick crowds and waves of people moving in all directions. I tried to move forward from the left side but was pushed back by crowds that were chanting:

"Down with the regime and Hosni Mubarak!"

I tried to circle around the central garden on the right side but was again pushed back by a group of Ultras who were carrying a huge Egyptian flag and chanting:

"He must leave! We won't leave!"

I found myself at the Talaat Harb entry point once more, so I contented myself with sitting on the green barrier and listening from a distance to the concert. I couldn't hear very clearly, so I made another attempt at moving closer to the stage. I stood on top of the stone plinth in the middle of the central garden of the midan, facing the effigy that was suspended from a lamppost. I smiled. This was a bit better. I could see a young man with a ponytail playing the guitar. He was saying:

"We want Hosni Mubarak to hear our voices."

He went on:

All of us, one hand, our demand, one stand:
Get out, get out, get out!

Down with, down with Hosni Mubarak!
Down with, down with Hosni Mubarak!
The people demand the removal of the regime!
The people demand the removal of the regime!

He must leave, we won't leave!
He must leave, we won't leave!

It was wonderful, despite the simplicity of the music. Bodies and flags were swaying and chanting. Fathers were carrying their children on their shoulders and moving them to the beat. Joy, happiness, and laughter. Music is magical. The audience asked the young man for an encore. He sang the song again; the audience got excited and started chanting, "Down with Hosni Mubarak." Then I heard the longest and loudest ululation blasting from the loudspeakers. A young couple was getting married in the midan. The largest zaffa in history started circling around the midan, a wedding procession accompanied by ululations, applause, whistling, and all kinds of chants. The young couple decided to spend the night in Tahrir. A tent was put up for them at the edge of the midan near Qasr al-Nil Bridge. I partied with the crowd until I was completely exhausted. I decided to go home. I wanted to sleep in my bed.

3

I slept for fourteen continuous and well-deserved hours. I took a real bath and then went to the hairdresser. Revolution does not mean that we must look bad and shabby. As I dressed up smartly, I remembered scenes from *The Lost City*, a film about the Cuban Revolution where the men's beards had grown disgustingly long and their clothes were all shabby, while the women looked unattractive and aggressive. I didn't want us to look like that. Looking good was important too.

"So where are you off to all dressed up like that?" my father asked admiringly.

"To Tahrir, of course."

"I thought you had a date!"

I laughed, "That's exactly what it is. I'm in love with Tahrir."

"So are you going to get your phone working now and give mine back?"

"I had forgotten! So you're sweet talking me because you want your phone back?"

"You've had it for the past ten days and I haven't opened my mouth."

"Okay. I'll go to Heliopolis before I go to Tahrir to get my old SIM card."

I gave him his phone and kissed him.

"Have lunch before you go. Your mother went shopping and will cook for you and your sister."

"I won't have enough time. I want to go to the midan before it gets dark. Au revoir!" And I waved.

"Au revoir! *Wa rahmatu l-llahi wa barakatu!*" he replied laughing, shaking his head in wonder.

I ran into my mother on my way down. I kissed her and took her shopping bags and walked her up quickly. I put them in front of the door to the apartment.

"Have lunch first. I'm making taro."

"Taro! You just broke my heart. I won't have enough time. Keep some for me for when I come back."

"The midan isn't going to disappear, you know!"

"It won't disappear but I miss it."

"Okay. Take good care of yourself and your sister."

"I will, promise."

I went to the Vodafone branch in Korba, Heliopolis, to activate my old SIM card. All the streets surrounding the Presidential Palace were closed to traffic. They had only left one narrow corridor open for pedestrians going into Korba, where they had their ID cards checked. The army was everywhere. The Presidential Guard was stationed behind the barbed wire next to the armored vehicles and tanks that surrounded the palace. Here, you could not have a conversation with any of the officers. You could only say good morning as you handed them your ID card. They responded curtly and without a smile. Life must have been very difficult for the residents of the neighborhood. The secret police were everywhere. I went to the Vodafone shop and waited for my turn. I looked at my watch; it was past noon. I mumbled, "I'm late going to the midan." I smiled at the way I said this to myself, as if I were late going to see my lover. Finally, I saw my number on the electronic screen above the head of one of the employees. I moved forward. I briefly told the employee about the SIM card I had lost during the demonstrations.

"Do you go to Tahrir?" he asked, smiling.

"Yes," I said, smiling back.

He handed me a new SIM card with the same number.

"How about you guys?"

"You can see how things are here," he said, signaling with his head toward the area outside the shop.

"So you go to Mostafa Mahmoud Mosque where his supporters are?" I said jokingly.

"Not at all! I've been to Tahrir twice. But I think we should let Mubarak finish his term. The country has come to a standstill. We used to close at 11 p.m. and now we close at 3 p.m., because of the curfew."

"It's okay. We're all in this together. We have to finish what we started. An unfinished revolution is Hell itself. An old man in the midan was carrying a sign saying this strapped across his chest."

The young man shook his head.

And I shrugged my shoulders.

"Thank you!"

I did not want to head back through the same route that was surrounded with barbed wire and the Presidential Guard. They were the part of the army I feared the most. I turned left into al-Ahram Street to get a cab. People were window-shopping, just like those only two hundred meters away from Tahrir, as if there wasn't a revolution going on in the country. I flagged down an old black-and-white cab.

"Tahrir? I mean Downtown."

"Please get in."

"Thank you."

"Are you going to Tahrir, ma'am?"

"Yes."

"I also go there every day."

"Really?"

"Of course. I wanted to see for myself and understand what exactly people wanted. I discovered that they're right."

"Good. So you didn't find any traitors or agents or people with their own agendas."

He laughed, "Not at all. And by the way, I also went to Mostafa Mahmoud. To be fair to both sides and to listen to what they had to say too."

"And what did you find?"

"Listen, ma'am, in all honesty, I found that Tahrir had more spirit and that its energy was more beautiful. The first time I went at midnight. I had no customers and the whole country was shut down because of the curfew, so I decided to go to Tahrir. A little while later, someone gave me a blanket, someone else gave me food, and another person was distributing juice. And to tell you the truth, my woman has been giving me Hell, because I'm not bringing in money. So, I started going to Tahrir every day at night and leaving in the morning. Sometimes, I would take people from Tahrir. I swear, I refused to take money from them. I would work all day, go home to see the kids and their mom, I'd give them their share of what I had made, I would rest a little and then go to Tahrir.

Laughing, I told the driver, "I like your story."

"I'm telling you the truth, but I think that people in Tahrir are right."

Finally, I arrived in Tahrir where there was life; there was death, as well, but not the boredom that I felt the minute I left the midan. I was greeted with huge posters of the martyrs. Some had been hung in the morning; others were carried by the families of the martyrs and their friends. I was moved as I looked at their youthful, determined faces. Black banners covered the corners of the posters. I recited the verses of the Fatiha to the memory of their souls. Please God, grant patience to their families; please help us get their rights. I continued strolling around the midan as I read the new banners that had been put up. A young man was carrying a sheet of white cardboard with a quotation from Gandhi: "First, they ignore you; then, they ridicule you; then, they fight you; then, you win." How eloquent and how expressive of what happened on January 25. Gandhi had most probably said this in the late thirties or early forties during the Indian struggle for independence against British colonialism. And there we were in 2011.

It seems that history does repeat itself, with minor changes, of course: regrettably, we are struggling against glorious Egyptian national rule not British colonialism. They have betrayed us. I saw an entire family whose members each carried a sign with one written word so that when standing together all the signs formed a sentence, "We came to kiss the feet of the youth of the revolution." A fully veiled woman was carrying a sign that read, "Egypt is for all Egyptians: Muslims and Christians." She had also drawn the crescent and the cross in an embrace. I was very happy. Egypt will always be well so long as Egyptians are aware that we are one people. A young man held up a sign that read, "It's been a week now, Mr. President, and not even a phone call." I laughed heartily. True, a week had already gone by since that last scandalous speech on Tuesday. He hadn't spoken to us again since. Another young man held up a caricature of a peasant complaining to the president and saying, "Mr. President, I sold the plot of land I owned to get my son a job." The president answered, "Man, I sold the whole country to get *my* son a job, and I still couldn't." Hilarious. The greatest thing was that people stopped to read each other's signs and take pictures as they showed off their own.

I spotted one of my friends coming from the direction of Qasr al-Nil Bridge.

"Wow! You look great!"

"So it shows! I went home and went to the hairdresser this morning. It's important that we look good. It's good for morale."

"So that's why I didn't find you at home this morning. Your mother answered the phone and said with pride that you and your sister were in Tahrir."

"Really? My mother was proud? Great! By the way, my old phone is working now."

"So I should call your old number?"

"Yeah."

"Okay, I'm going home now. I've been here since 9 a.m. I'll see you tomorrow."

"Okay, sweetie."

I walked in the direction of Qasr al-Nil Street to go to Merit to see my friends. The citizens' checkpoint, whose members I knew, stopped me at the entry point. One of them asked me to help search the women and girls who had queued in front of them. I happily agreed. It seemed like they were a group of women from a Christian charity organization. They were all wearing green T-shirts and crosses. They looked like they were from Heliopolis. I smiled at them and to myself. I had thought that there was no hope in the residents of Heliopolis. One of them said, "We are here to join you."

"Welcome! Which organization do you belong to?"

"We don't belong to an organization. We just got together and started thinking about what the midan might need. And we decided that we would collect the garbage. We hired a garbage truck to take it all out of the midan."

"Thank you so much! True, the midan is full of garbage now."

I checked their ID cards and handbags. The younger girls didn't have IDs.

"Do you have a school ID or a club membership card?"

"Sure."

They all walked through with big, thick, black garbage bags. They were all wearing gloves and masks. They began collecting the garbage and putting it in the truck they had hired.

I went to Merit to see friends and rest for a while. I chatted with some who were stretching out and taking a break like me. We watched the news on TV. Nothing worth talking about.

I went back to the midan to my position on Talaat Harb Street. I greeted my friends in the organization committee and stood beside Emad. I put my arm around his shoulder.

"How are you doing?"

"Good, and you?"

"Good."

"You look very pretty today."

I gave him a big smile.

A group of friends came by with a couple of foreign journalists who asked to interview us. I introduced them to Emad. He told his story and I translated it. He told the story passionately, despite how painful it all was. The journalists praised him for his courage. I felt proud just standing there by his side.

A veiled woman stopped in front of me.

"I want to donate money, but I don't know who to give it to."

"Actually, I don't know who is collecting donations."

"So, can I give you the money and you decide what's needed?"

She handed me several one-hundred-pound bills.

"We really don't need anything. We have juice, food, water, and medicine."

"Please, see what might still be missing."

Suddenly, I remembered the socks I had not changed for days before going back home.

"Socks! I'll buy socks. And maybe some razor blades."

"Thank you so much. I really wanted to help in any way I could."

"Thank you."

I then produced my ID card and showed it to her.

"No need for that. I trust you."

"Still, so that you know who you gave your money to."

She refused to look at my ID card and smiled as she walked away.

I looked for socks among the peddlers in the midan but couldn't find one who sold any. Usually, there were loads of them, calling out three pairs for ten pounds. I asked one of the peddlers, and he pointed one out on Talaat Harb Street. I bought two hundred pounds worth of socks for starters and went back to the central garden of the midan. I went around the tents where families and groups of young people were chatting. Some were making tea and others were making sandwiches. Kids were running around. It was life in all its details.

"Socks, guys? Only for those who are spending the night."

"Thanks!"

I could sense their hesitation.

"They're for free. Gifts."

"Really? Great. Could we have a pair here, and another one there?"

I handed out thirty pairs of socks in five minutes. I went back to the vendor and bought some more with the money I had left. I distributed them in a different area in the midan.

I passed in front of KFC and discovered a group of barbers who were cutting men's hair and shaving their beards. They had a sign that read, "Barber of the Revolution, Free."

I quickly went up to Pierre's apartment and grabbed my camera and took pictures of them as we joked together.

"You should have come yesterday before I went to the hairdresser."

"Sorry about that. We were thinking of how we might contribute to the revolution in a practical way. By the time we got together . . . ."

"Where are you from?"

"Some are from Sheikh Zayed, others from Dar al-Salam and Helwan."

"We are very grateful. We really need barbers in the midan."

I resumed my walk in the midan, then joined a group that had lit a fire and gathered around it. They were singing an Abdel Halim Hafez song, "Sura, sura, sura / Kullina kida awzin sura."

We sang, clapped, danced, and laughed till dawn.

4

I had a dream about Cairo airport. The VIP lounge and unusual commotion: people running, airplanes taking off. Will he run away like Zein al-Abedin?

Thousands flocked to the midan from all directions, chanting:

"Leave now, you thick-skinned cow!"

The midan was witnessing another million-man march. The people inside the midan welcomed the arriving crowds with cheers and applause. Several broadcasting stations inside the midan were playing, "Ya habibti ya Masr" and "Helwa baladi al-samra." Everyone was singing along enthusiastically and joyfully. I moved along in the circular direction of the midan. I looked at the smiling, hopeful faces and read the different signs. A young man held a sign that read, "Leave already! I miss my fiancée"; another was holding his cat with a sign around her neck that read, "No Mubarak." I laughed aloud. That's a new one! Children on their parents' shoulders were waving the flags in their hands. A little girl held onto her mother with one hand and grasped a sign with the other that read, "I Understand." Men were walking in the midan carrying their shrouds; others had taped their mouths shut. No more talk before departure. An older man hung a sign around his neck that read: "Leave. My woman wants to give birth and the kid doesn't want to see you." A blind man in traditional clothes was feeling his way with a stick toward the central garden in search of an empty spot where he could sit. People made way for him and welcomed him. He took off his shoes, crossed his legs on the ground and started swaying his body as Qur'an reciters do; then, he started improvising:

"*Bismillah al-Rahman al-Rahim*. The revolutionaries are in the right. The people demand the removal of the regime. The revolutionaries have spoken the truth."

"Allah, Allah, how beautiful!"

People praised him and greeted him warmly, and some offered him tea and cigarettes.

I looked at the man admiringly, even though he could not see me, and then went on with my morning tour.

Someone stopped me and greeted me very warmly.

"How are you?"

"I'm fine," I said, as I looked at him with surprise.

"Don't you remember me?"

"I'm sorry, but . . . . ."

"I'm the nurse at al-Raai al-Saleh clinic. I'm the one who . . . ."

"Yes, yes. Now I remember."

I smiled when I remembered that this same man had wanted to die. "This is my son."

He introduced me to a young man whose arm was in a cast.

"Hello, my dear. I hope you get well soon."

"I came to the midan after my son was injured during the Battle of the Camel. Since then, I come here after work every day. You were right."

"I'm really happy that you're here with us. It's great to have you in the midan."

"It's great to have you here too!"

We said goodbye and went our different ways amid the crowds.

I shook my head as I walked along, smiling and happy to have met this man. He had been so gloomy at the clinic. What a change!

Anyone who looked at our faces now would have been amazed. I was amazed. We used to look pale, sickly, and depressed. When someone told a joke, people would laugh but not from the heart. They didn't even laugh; they just allowed their lips to part in a faint and hesitant smile. Now, our faces were radiating joy, hope, and good health. Even the families of the martyrs had regained their smiles, their strength, and their determination, despite their grief, for us to live, for us to have a better, more human life.

I walked toward the entrance to Tahrir, near the Egyptian Museum. I stood with the organization committee members and followed the arrival of different delegations: a delegation of families from Munufiya (the governorate Mubarak is from) held a big sign that read, "Your Birth-place Wants Your Head." They were followed by a delegation from Sinai with a sign that read, "I'm From Sinai and I'm Set on Your Departure." One of the young men in the organization committee came toward me and politely asked that I help with searching the women.

"If you don't mind, we need someone who does not wear the face veil because some of the ladies don't like being searched by veiled women."

"No problem. True, it's not easy to be searched by someone whose face you can't see. I'll help with great pleasure."

I stood with the women and we got organized. I asked the two veiled helpers to check IDs and bags, while I gently felt the women's veils and their pockets in search of any sharp objects. Then, I would apologize for the inconvenience with a smile. More delegations arrived from different governorates. They split at the barrier: one queue for the women and another for the men. Then, they would meet up again after the barrier. The delegation from Aswan was carrying a banner that read, "We Have Come from Aswan; No to Mubarak and No to Suleiman." The greatest thing about these banners and signs was their attention to rhyme and their sense of humor, of course. Enter the del-egation from Port Said, with a straightforward banner that read, "Get the Hell Out! May Our Country See the Light." Port Said was one of the cities that had most reason to be angry with Mubarak, since the incident of the man who tried to give Mubarak a message, but was mis-taken by the Presidential Guard for someone attempting to assassinate the president, and was shot dead. God bless his soul. One has come to doubt many things. Perhaps even the assassination attempt in Addis Ababa was a bluff.

Rumors circulated in the midan that Mubarak was leaving for Germany for health reasons. No one confirmed the news and no one refuted it.

There were mass resignations within the ranks of the NDP.

Meetings took place between representatives of the Muslim Broth-erhood and Omar Suleiman, which were frowned upon by people in the midan.

The employees of the Egyptian Communications Authority joined the people in Tahrir.

The residents of Kharga in al-Wadi al-Gadid demanded the intervention of the minister of the interior, having been attacked with teargas and birdshot during demonstrations.

So this country has finally figured out that there's a revolution?

I went back to my position on Talaat Harb Street, sat down on the sidewalk, and stretched out my legs. My feet were aching after standing for so long. Two members from the organization committee halfway down the street approached, holding a man whose body was swaying as he shouted, "I love Mubarak." I laughed, so did the army soldiers, the officers, and the passersby. He was a middle-aged man in a faded coat worn over a dirty shirt and a pair of gray pants. He was unshaven, with drunken eyes but a smiley face. The young men handed him over to the army personnel. He had a bottle of wine in his hand and was saying persistently:

"Yes! I love Mubarak."

"Okay, man, love him, but do it somewhere else."

One of the officers took the bottle of wine from him and gave him juice instead. He sat him down.

"Have mercy on Mubarak. Let me into the midan, so I can explain to people."

We all laughed aloud despite ourselves.

"We're concerned for you. If we let you into the midan they're going to beat you to death."

"Calm down and go home."

"Or go to Mostafa Mahmoud . . . . Mubarak's people are there."

"I love Mubarak!"

More laughter.

"What to do? The guy has gone mad!"

One of the officers took him by the hand and walked away, as we continued to laugh at him.

I went to Pierre's apartment. I wanted to see the multitudes in the midan from upstairs. The balcony was crammed with photographers, journalists, friends, and acquaintances. I squeezed in among them to take pictures. The midan looked like a huge star that was filled to the last inch with tents in the middle. The Egyptian flag fluttered everywhere.

People circled the midan, as they did the Kaaba. Another concert began, but I would not have been able to get to where it was, as I had done a couple of days ago. I decided to stay where I was and rest my feet. One of the young men shouted, "The tables have turned!"

"What happened?"

"Breaking news: they say the thugs in Port Said burned down the governorate building."

"Why did they burn it down?"

"Because the NDP guys who hired them to beat the protestors and break up the demonstrations had promised them government apartments and didn't deliver."

"The thugs said we've done our job and they fooled us."

"Sweet! They deserve it."

"So the thugs are now going to join the revolution!"

"Why not!"

Ululations rose through the loudspeakers in the midan. Another wedding and another historic zaffa. We cheered and ululated along in celebration, as much as we could from the balcony, as we waved our flags.

5

The call for dawn prayer in a beautiful, serene, quiet voice could be heard from the minaret of Omar Makram Mosque. If only all calls to prayer had this dignified effect. I thank God that I am far from the mosque right next door to our house where, as soon as the caller has the microphone in hand, he begins shouting out the prayer. As if there was no other way but a loud, distorted voice to bring you closer to God and spread His word. I made myself some Nescafé with milk and sat on the balcony, watching the sunrise. There was quiet movement in the midan: some were going to pray, others were making tea, while others still queued in front of the peddlers' handcarts for couscous, fuul, and sweet potato. Serenity reigned over the midan. I started humming "al-Helwa" by Sayyid Darwish.

Several older images of the midan crossed my mind, images from my childhood with my parents and sister, the green pedestrian bridge that used to surround the midan. We used to walk up its steps to get from one side of the midan to the other. There used to be a big fountain in the middle that sprinkled our faces with water when we came close to it on summer days, laughing. There was a huge clock-shaped flower arrangement in the garden of the Mugammaa that actually worked. The parking lot for public buses was in front of the museum. These were big red buses that had numbers with a dash and others without. The electric trams on Qasr al-Aini Street often stopped due to power cuts and blocked traffic on the street, so that cars and buses had to drive around them. The stone base in the middle of the midan was intended for a statue that was never erected—I think it may have been for a statue of Khedive Ismail. Omar Effendi department store sat on the corner of Suleiman Pasha Street (now Talaat Harb); it had an escalator, perhaps the very first one in Egypt. I used to be very frightened of it and thought that the demons themselves operated it. I used to hold onto my mother's hand with my feet glued to the ground. I would scream in fear and people around us would laugh at me.

The midan used to look quite different. Now it looked different again, with the tents and the shabby shelters and food and popcorn handcarts. At first sight, these human masses looked inharmonious. The midan looked like one of those informal neighborhoods. I smiled to myself and to the midan and to the new day.

I went out to say good morning to those who were up. I walked across Qasr al-Nil Bridge and stopped once midway to look at the river. I pleaded with the water, the sky, and the wind—all the elements of the earth—that we be granted victory. I sat on the sidewalk and lit a cigarette. Two young men nearby invited me to have tea with them. I smiled and took a glass from one of them.

"Thank you."

I held the glass with both hands to warm my cold fingers.

One of them said, "I think I saw you yesterday."

Under normal circumstances, I would have ignored this kind of comment and would have considered it flirtatious or a trick to start up a conversation, like asking for the time for example. Instead, I smiled and told him that I had been in the midan since January 25.

"I work in the Emirates. I couldn't believe my eyes when I saw the demonstrations on TV on January 25. I wanted to be with you, even to die with the martyrs on the 28th. I got on the first flight back to Egypt."

"Welcome back. These are the most beautiful days of our lives."

"I don't know how to put it, but it feels that this revolution has given us back our dignity. Can you believe that my Emirati employers came to congratulate me when I'm just a worker? It's the first time I've felt proud to be Egyptian."

His voice faltered as his eyes filled with tears. I had tears in my eyes too.

"I love Egypt very much, but I had no job and couldn't get an apartment to get married in and all that. Now, I want to come back and start over here. All the others who were on the flight with me were saying the same thing. We were all happy, chanting, 'Raise your head up high, you're an Egyptian,' on the plane and at the airport," he said as he wiped away the tears that rolled down his face.

"We will all rebuild a clean Egypt together. Now, there is meaning and hope—hope in the future."

I thanked him for the tea and left.

"I'll see you in the midan."

Huge crowds were advancing on Qasr al-Nil Bridge on their way to Tahrir. I joined the queue at the entrance to the midan and prepared my ID for the checkpoint. I walked toward Omar Makram Mosque and then decided to continue walking to the Parliament. There was a military checkpoint at the entrance to the street. The officer I had flirted with when the army first arrived in the midan smiled at me.

"Please come through, Professor."

I gave him my ID card.

"No need, really."

"Thank you for your graciousness, but this is the right thing to do."

He had to take the ID. He checked it quickly and returned it to me.

"Believe me, if you were to try to walk through in civilian clothes, I would still ask to check your ID," I said, laughing.

The officer laughed and nodded in agreement.

"From now on, there will be no cutting corners."

The army soldiers laughed. I waved goodbye as I walked through.

I walked behind the Mugammaa building to Qasr al-Aini Street then to Maglis al-Shaab Street—the People's Assembly Street. Someone had crossed out the name of the street with black paint and had written "The People's Street" instead. Hundreds of people were sitting on the ground and some had put up tents. I had no idea that some protestors had moved out here. I had thought that the space was closed. Many banners and posters hung on the gates and walls of the Parliament. At one gate, the poster read, "Entrance Gate for Their Excellencies the Thieves." At another gate, another poster read, "Entrance Gate for the VIP Thieves." I laughed aloud as I continued to walk among the people. The laughter became contagious and everyone started laughing as I pointed to the posters. Egyptians are so funny!

I went back to the midan, feeling proud that I belonged to this remarkable, civilized, and historic people. It was very crowded in front of the radio station at Hardee's. I stood with the crowds to listen to the latest news: a call for a general strike across the country and news of demonstrations by the workers of the Electricity Company. They were chanting, "He must leave! We won't leave!" in front of the company headquarters. Thousands of workers from petroleum companies were on strike in front of the Ministry of Petroleum; the employees of the Red Crescent were demonstrating, so were those in the Water Supply Company, the employees of the Postal Services in Ataba, the garbage collectors on Sudan Street, and many others. This was amazing. The crowds cheered and chanted, "Allahu Akbar!"

Omar Suleiman had deemed the Egyptian people not ready for democracy. He should shut his mouth and come to Tahrir to see for himself. And, my God, have we it with that Shafiq who had wanted to give the demonstrators candy. How idiotic.

Thousands of striking employees and workers arrived in Tahrir to participate in the open sit-in. This is the beginning of the end, Mubarak. I didn't want to leave the midan, but it was my father's birthday.

I called my sister so that we could go home together. She was in the vicinity of Maglis al-Shaab Street. We agreed to meet at the Isaaf metro station. At home, we had lunch with our parents. My mother had baked a cake for my father's birthday.

"Your birthday, Baba, has come during momentous days! The days of the revolution."

My father laughed and seemed pleased with my comment and with our being there with him. My sister decided to spend the evening at home with my father, whereas I quickly changed my clothes and got ready to leave.

"Why so fast? Stay a little."

"Sorry, Baba."

I didn't know how to tell him that the midan had become my home.

"I want to get there before curfew."

"Okay. Look after yourself."

"Happy birthday to the greatest father in the world! My you live to be two hundred thousand years old!

He laughed, "That's all I get from you!"

I hugged and kissed him, and he held me tight. I hugged and kissed my mother. She embraced me back, with her lips pursed in distaste.

I waited at the bus stop. A couple of minutes later, the bus rolled in slowly and the ticket collector called out, "Ramsis, Tahrir, Demonstrations."

My face lit up.

"Are you for the demonstrations?"

"Of course! And tomorrow we're going on strike."

"Long live the drivers and ticket collectors of public transportation. Good on you!"

On the way, the ticket collector continued to call out, "Ramsis, Tahrir, Demonstrations."

All those who got on the bus were indeed going to Tahrir for the demonstrations.

There was not an inch left in the midan for new arrivals. Even though the capacity of the midan should only allow half a million people, miraculously, it seemed to accommodate two million, if not more. There was no need anymore to call for another million-man march, for millions were going out of their own accord in many public squares: Tahrir, al-Arbein, al-Qaid Ibrahim, and many others in different cities. All your public squares, Egypt, have become Tahrir.

Everywhere in the midan people were chanting, "The people demand the removal of the regime!"

6

Morning brought more strikes, more sit-ins, and more demonstrations in all governorates. Finally, the Egyptian people have awakened and are demanding their rights. Tahrir seemed to expand all the way down to

Qasr al-Nil Bridge, to accommodate the thousands that continued to arrive. There was an overwhelming feeling that victory was just around the corner. Rumors that Mubarak had left the country spread: some said that he had gone to the Emirates, some said Sharm al-Sheikh; two days earlier, the rumor had been that he had gone to Germany. I suddenly remembered my dream: the unusual commotion at Cairo Airport and the VIP lounge. But could he have just taken off without delivering his third speech in which he would say, "Now I understand you, now I understand you"? How could you take off without understanding, Mr. President?

"Mubarak will not leave until we have a zaar to dispel him."

"A zaar!"

"He's like a demon that will only leave if we get the blue jinn to drive him out!"

I couldn't help giggling. A group of men and young protestors started beating drums and tambourines. It was incredible. Egyptians are really something else.

"Go, go . . . my love, . . . go on, my love. Go, go . . . go on, my love."

The men circled around a young man who was wearing a red Santa-like hood on his head and was swaying his arms to the left and to the right, like a dervish. They chanted and swayed their bodies like him. Many other people joined the circle and were laughing and chanting along with them: "Go, go." News of the zaar circulated in the midan. Many liked the idea and reproduced it in other circles with different variations. Some chanted, "Leave," while others chanted, "Go." The midan was transformed into a moulid, a carnival. We were only missing the swings for the kids.

My phone rang, but I couldn't see the number of the caller.

"Hello?"

"Hello!"

I immediately recognized the voice, one that I had not heard for a very long time.

"It's you!"

"Yes, it's me!"

I laughed.

"You think you're the only ones who ever had a revolution? We haven't been getting any sleep because of you!"

"Have you been following?"

"Yes. The TV is on 24/7. How are you doing?"

"I'm fine. I'm happy. How about you? When is your revolution?"

"Hahaha. No, we don't do that kind of stuff."

"That's what we used to say here too!"

"I'm glad you're well. I just wanted to make sure that you're okay."

"Thanks a lot for the phone call. Thanks to the revolution that reminded you of me. This is the third revolutionary gain!"

"So what are the other two?"

"I got an iPhone as a present to replace the one that State Security took from me, and I've lost six kilos!"

"So by the time I come, you will be nothing but bones?"

"No, you will find a revolutionary model!"

"You take care now."

"I will."

What an eventful day! This phone call made me optimistic. So much good was coming my way. I was elated.

A man passed by with a very funny sign. It seemed that he was a teacher. The sign was a mock school certificate for the student Mohamed Hosni Mubarak. He had failed in all of his subjects: health services, education, industry, agriculture, commerce. Red circles surrounded the failing zero signs and the certificate was stamped with the official stamp of the republic. I saluted the man holding the sign in appreciation. It was an ingenious idea. Tough luck, Hosni, but you brought it all upon yourself.

I sat on the green barrier on Talaat Harb Street, watching what was taking place in the midan. Students and university professors from Qasr al-Aini medical school, including dentists and pharmacists, were marching in their white coats toward the midan on Qasr al-Aini Street. They were followed by lawyers and judges in their black robes, coming from the direction of Abdel Moneim Riyad. A group of young people were unrolling a very long banner made of cloth. Some got onto each other's shoulders and started scaling the lampposts that were close to the central garden. They hung up the banner that read, "The people have already removed the regime." People cheered and applauded joyfully. It's true that the president had not yet stepped down, but the people had already taken the decision. The radio station at Hardee's broadcast Abdel Rahman al-Abnoudi's latest poem "al-Midan." He had written it for us, for the people of the midan. Despite the chanting and the noise, I could still make out some of the verses in al-Abnoudi's voice:

> Oh state of old men, your time is now done.
> You ravaged our lands, rabid and old.
> One like the other, in greed, filth, and mold.
> Wondrous buds bloomed, turned fall into spring,
> Raising the dead, the miracle youth can bring.
> Shoot me! My murder won't bring back your state.
> For my people, I write in my blood a new fate.
> My blood or the spring, both they are green.
> I smile—in joy or sorrow, remains to be seen.
> . . . .
> Is this not the same youth we had accused of hating their country?
> Did we not dress in black and move away from them?
> Today they are the ones who ignited revolution,
> Sorting those who supported them and those who betrayed them.
> Here's to the midan that embraced the idea and wrought it.
> Here's to the midan that enchanted people with its magic.
> Here's to the midan whose name was for so long eclipsed but was none-
> theless patient,
> Between those who adored and those who hated.
> Youth . . . as if the midan were their family and abode.
> There is no Nescafé or cappuccino there.
> Youth whose cheeks came to know the beauty of sleeping on asphalt.
> Death knows them well and they know death too.
> Oh people, injustice is not easy and these youth are not children.
> No matter how they try to besiege the midan it will always defy.

Oh Abnoudi, how beautiful!

Suddenly, I was overtaken by a desire to watch Egyptian state TV. I wanted to know what they were airing and how they were representing the midan. So I went to Merit. As usual, it was like a beehive, but it seemed that some like me had the same sinful desire: they were watching the Nile News channel. But there was no live coverage from the midan. The anchorman was receiving phone calls.

"The country is in ruins! And we are responsible for that. History will tell that we destroyed our country. Oh God! No, no, no. It's not us, dear God," the caller wailed.

"What is this? Why is he doing this?" asked one of the people watching the show.

"Excuse me, please, are you saying that the groups inside are not allowing people to leave the midan? Could you tell us more about the groups inside? Are they Egyptian or foreign? Do you know which nationalities?"

"They are foreigners who speak good English. They all speak English inside the midan. They are with us all the time. They took part in the demonstrations and supported our demands. They made the flyers with us. But now, the ones who are making the calls inside the midan are Egyptian. Tomorrow's slogan is 'Friday of Deliverance.' Deliverance from what?" the caller asked, whimpering.

"I really appreciate this, Mr. Tamer. But may I please ask you a favor?"

"Yes," he replied, still moaning.

"You are in Ghamra right now, yes?"

"Yes. It wasn't easy trying to contact you. Not everyone is able to contact you."

"Listen to me, Mr. Tamer. You are in Ghamra, right?

"Exactly."

Most of us laughed at the mediocrity of the performance.

"Please, I am making this request in front of all Egyptians. Please come to the Nile channel offices, so we can talk about this together. Please call my colleagues so they can bring you to the control room."

"You are making this even more difficult for me," he responded, still whining.

"No, not at all. I'm not making it difficult."

"No, no, I can't."

"Please, do come and talk to us here. We need to have everyone hear you, because you are a case from inside the midan, and everyone needs to know what is happening inside, because most of the people and other satellite channels don't know what is happening inside. And you know as well as everyone else that tonight will be a very sensitive night. We want to know what is happening inside. We want to hear it from you. Is there anyone inside who actually cares for Egypt? Anyone who cares for the country? Did anyone feel that they were put in a compromised position? Please, accept our invitation."

"For my sake, please try to get inside the midan with your cameras," Mr. Tamer said, still whimpering.

"We will. We will."

"The place is on fire."

"See how the dirty Egyptian media is inciting people against us? Hosting someone to provoke people."

"He reminded me of the woman who called in to ask for protection from the thugs. Same kind of performance."

"This guy has excelled in his dramatic performance."

"What a farce!"

"The real disaster is that people actually believe this drivel."

"Tamer from Ghamra!"

Calls were already circulating on Facebook for the Friday of Deliverance. There were also calls for a march to the Presidential Palace in Heliopolis. I was not for the march to the Presidential Palace. I feared the Presidential Guard. I had seen them from a distance when I was in Heliopolis, standing on top of their armored vehicles, in front of the palace quite aloof from the people. They were not like the officers and soldiers we talked to and drank tea and smoked with. I couldn't make up my mind if this was the right or wrong thing to do. I went back to the entrance of Talaat Harb and told the officers standing there, with whom we had developed a close relationship, about the idea of the march to the palace.

"Do you think the Presidential Guard out there will attack us?"

"Possibly," answered an unpleasant officer who had recently joined the group.

"Should I post this on Facebook?"

"Yes, go ahead and post it."

"What is your name so I can use it as a reference?"

"No. Don't mention my name."

"Is this your personal opinion, then? If it is, please keep it to yourself."

I looked at him with disgust and walked away.

I went to Pierre's apartment. It was very crowded in front of the TV.

"What's happening?"

"A statement from the Supreme Council of the Armed Forces announcing that it is in a state of permanent session."

"Oh, really? Is that all?"

"The footage they showed was without Mubarak."

"What does that mean? Is there going to be a coup?"

"I'm not sure, but it looks like it."

"Anyway, I have no problem with the army taking over for a while, until things settle down and we can have a civilian president."

"If the army takes over, it won't stay for a while, it will stay forever. They have ruled us since 1952, even if they gave up their military outfits for civilian clothes."

"Come on, guys, let's not be pessimistic, please."

"This is not pessimism. It's reality."

I went out on the balcony and looked out at the volatile situation in the midan. People were chanting with determination, "The people have already removed the regime!" The chanting reached us on the ninth floor with the same power and determination.

This people will not be defeated.

"Guys, Mubarak will deliver a speech in a little while," shouted one of those watching TV.

"This is the third speech, guys. Get it?"

"He must be seeing the two million in Tahrir, the one and a half million in Alexandria, and the thousands of protestors in the other governorates."

"Hope he's not watching the Egyptian state channels!"

"That would be a real disaster!"

A feeling of victory reigned over the midan as news of Mubarak's third speech began to circulate. The patriotic song "Bismillah" rose in the sky, and the crowds gathered around the giant TV screen in front of Hardee's and the other screens in the midan.

The Third Speech

People and youth of Egypt, I am addressing you today; I am addressing the youth of Egypt in Tahrir Square and throughout Egypt; I am addressing you today with a speech from the heart. A speech of a father to his sons and daughters.

I would like to tell you that I am proud of you as a symbol of a new genera-tion of Egyptians that is calling for change for the better, is committed to this change, and is dreaming of and making a better future.

Laughter erupted.

I would like to tell you that my response to your voice, to your message, to your demands, is an irrevocable commitment, and I am absolutely determined to fulfill what I have promised you with all seriousness and honesty. And I am completely committed to implementing all of this without hesitation.

More laughter.

Youth of Egypt, sons of Egypt, brothers, citizens, I have expressed with all clarity my intention not to stand for the forthcoming elections. I have already served this country for more than sixty years, in peace and war. I express my commitment to this, and I express a similar pledge and commitment to carry on—to shoulder my responsibility to protect the constitution and the interests of the people, until power and responsibility can be transferred to whoever is elected by voters next September, in fair and free elections that will be guaran-teed to be transparent and free. This is the pledge that I made before God and the nation. And I will safeguard this pledge, until together we take Egypt and its people to the shore of safety.

"No way! You still want to stay until September?"

"F—k you!"

"Leave! Leave!"

The chant rose from the midan. We ran out onto the balcony. The crowds were holding up their shoes to the TV screens. "Leave!" Just one word. "Leave!" All of us together, in one breath.

"This crazy guy! He can't bring himself to step down."

We have, in fact, started a very constructive national dialogue that includes Egypt's youth and all the political forces who have led the call for change. This dialogue has resulted in a preliminary rapprochement of opinions and positions, which has put us at the beginning of the right path to overcome this crisis. And we should carry on this dialogue so as translate it into a real plan—a clear roadmap, within a precise and fixed timeframe that, over the coming days, would ensure a peaceful transition of power, starting now and continuing until September.

"F—k you!"

"Leave! Leave! Leave!"

Like the youth of Egypt today, I was a young man as well when I joined the military and when I pledged loyalty to the nation and sacrificed for it. I spent my life defending Egypt's land and sovereignty. I saw its wars, its defeats, and its victories. I lived through days of occupation and frustration and days of liberation. Those were the best days. The best day of my life was when I raised the flag of Egypt over Sinai. I confronted death several times as a pilot and then in Addis Ababa. I never gave in to foreign pressures. I have protected peace and worked hard for Egypt's stability. I have worked hard for Egypt's progress and the progress of its people. I never sought power or false popularity. I believe that the majority of the Egyptian people know who Hosni Mubarak is, and it pains me to hear what has been expressed by some people from my own country.

"You want our pity now? 'It pains me!' indeed! May you burn in Hell."

I am aware of the dangers facing us at this difficult juncture, and I believe that Egypt is going through a very significant phase in its history. This compels all to put the interests of the nation first and put Egypt above any consideration. I have decided to delegate powers of the president to the vice president, according to the constitution.

"F—k you!"

"Omar Suleiman? Delegate to Omar Suleiman? What does this mean?"

"Leave! Leave! Leave!"

Once again, I would like to say that I have lived for the sake of this nation—to protect it and be responsible for it and its well-being. Egypt will prevail above all.

"Leave! Leave! Leave!"

I went out to the midan. The radio station at Hardee's was calling on doctors to come to the stage. There had been several cases of heart failure, fainting, and nervous attacks. Damn you, Mubarak. May you burn as you have burned our hearts tonight. If you are not tried for every-thing you've done in the past, you must be tried for this speech. What do you want? You want more blood? You want destruction till the very last minute? If you really love this country, leave. Leave!

Tears came rolling down my face. My feet grew heavy as I watched old women and men weeping and young protestors knocking their heads against the walls. People carried each other and asked for doctors. Immediate collective decision: march to the TV Building in Maspero and to the Presidential Palace. Someone on the stage asked people to remain in the midan. But thousands began to head toward Maspero, while others started to march to Heliopolis. I could not do a thing. I went to Pierre's apartment and collapsed in a chair.

14
February 11,
Friday of Deliverance

I woke up at dawn. I looked around me to determine where I was. I was still in the chair I had collapsed into some hours before. Despair, depression, and confusion covered the faces of those present. I decided to go to Maspero. I wanted to find out how those who had gone were doing. I wrapped a small blanket around my shoulders and took off.

I could hear the defiant chant "Leave," before even arriving in Maspero. Thousands were gathered in front of the TV Building where army and Presidential Guard armored vehicles were lined up. Since last night, thousands had been chanting one word in the same breath, "Leave!" I met some of my friends, but we did not speak. We had nothing to say. All we could do was chant with the people, "Leave!"

We remained in this state until mid-morning when waves of people began arriving from all directions. The Corniche was filled with people coming from Shubra and Maadi. I went back to Pierre's apartment to report on the situation in Maspero. I made tea for myself and others and went out onto the balcony. My Armenian friend called to tell me that thousands of Heliopolis residents were marching to the Presidential Palace and had joined those arriving from Tahrir. He was with them.

"Really?"

I repeated the news aloud to those standing with me.

"Heliopolis has joined, guys!"

He told me that others I knew were also there.

"Incredible! They were against the revolution to begin with."

"But after last night's speech, they said this won't work anymore."

"You make me want to come to Heliopolis."

"If you want to come, take the Salah Salem Road and then Marghani."

"Why?'

"Because the road is blocked at Heliopolis Club and Korba."

"Okay, I'll think about it. I don't know if I can walk all that distance."

I considered joining the chic residents of Heliopolis. I wanted to see girls and women whose hair had been styled at the hairdressers and who were wearing fancy clothes—a change from the shabbiness of Tahrir. What is this classist thinking, Mona! No I won't go to Heliopolis. I will remain with the people.

One of the people in front of the TV announced that there would be a statement by the Military Council. We quickly went inside to watch.

Due to successive developments in the current situation, which define the destiny of the country, and in the context of ongoing monitoring of internal and external incidents and the decision to delegate responsibilities to the vice president of the country, and in the belief that it is our national responsibility to preserve the stability and safety of the nation ...

"It's the same one they broadcast last night after the stupid speech."

"I didn't watch it."

... the Supreme Council of the Armed Forces has decided:

First, to secure the implementation of the following: Ending the state of emergency as soon as the current circumstances are over; deciding on the appeals against elections and taking consequent measures; and conducting the necessary legislative amendments and holding free and fair presidential elections, in light of approved constitutional amendments.

Second, the armed forces are committed to sponsoring the legitimate demands of the people and achieving them by following the implementation of these procedures, in the defined time frames and with utmost accuracy and seriousness, until the peaceful transfer of authority is completed, leading to the free, democratic community to which the people aspire.

Third, the armed forces emphasize the security forces will not pursue the honest people who rejected corruption and demanded reform, and warns against any infringement of the security and safety of the nation and the people. It also emphasizes the need for regular work in state facilities and the return to normal life to preserve the interests and property of our great people.

God protect the nation and the people.

"So what does this mean? What does it mean that they have delegated to the vice president?"

"I don't know. But at least they acknowledged the people's legitimate rights."

"And people are demanding the removal of the regime. I don't understand a thing."

A friend of mine who was in Maspero called and asked me to help at the checkpoint.

"The numbers are big! And we are many but still not enough."

"Okay."

I wanted to run there, but the crowds slowed me down. Finally, I arrived and stood with my friends to help search the women who were arriving from Shubra. I suddenly realized that the Friday sermon had started. I wanted to listen to what the sheikh was going to say, but I couldn't make out his words. The Friday prayer began. The protestors lined up along the entire length of the street and the sidewalk of the Corniche. The officers and soldiers lined up behind the barbed wire. When I saw the officers praying, I felt optimistic. As soon as the prayer ended, before the second 'salam' that brings the prayer to a close, the demonstrators started chanting, "Leave!" My feet were tired from having stood for so long, so I asked one of the women to replace me and I went and sat on the sidewalk. One of the more senior officers, perhaps a general, appeared in the midst of the protestors. People rushed toward him and so did I. I wanted to ask him about the statement that the Supreme Council of the Armed Forces had issued. I was finally able to catch up with him.

"Excuse me sir, I have a question please."

"Go ahead," he replied impatiently.

"I listened to the statement but didn't quite understand it."

"What didn't you understand? The statement was very clear," he replied with irritation.

"I mean, what are we supposed to do?"

"You should leave," he said, as he hurried away.

I hurried behind him and held him by the arm.

"Excuse me, but where should we go?"

"Go home," he said, as he walked away from me.

I stood there for a moment trying to grasp what the general had just said. Go home? I was being pushed back to Tahrir with the movement of the crowds.

I continued shuttling between Tahrir and Maspero, Pierre's apartment and Merit throughout the whole day. I just couldn't stay put.

My Armenian friend called to tell me that there were some fifty thousand demonstrators at the Presidential Palace and near Heliopolis Club and that the women were showering the officers with roses.

"Wait, wait."

"What is it?"

"The tanks are moving their turrets. Oh God! Are they going to fire at us?"

A pause.

"No. They've changed the direction. Now, they're pointed toward the palace."

"No way. Thank God. Does this mean that the Presidential Guard is on our side?"

The anxiety that had overtaken me since the day before subsided. Thank God. I walked through Qasr al-Nil Street into the alley that led to Estoril restaurant and then to Talaat Harb Street.

Allah Akbar! Allah Akbar! Long live Egypt! Long live Egypt! He stepped down. He stepped down!

People were shouting and cheering on the street. I asked one of the people who was shouting "Allahu Akbar," and he said, "He stepped down! Mubarak stepped down!"

"Are you sure? It might be a rumor."

"The statement is on TV," he replied, pointing at a small screen in front of one of the shops.

I couldn't see or hear anything because of the crowds.

People were hugging each other, jumping up and down, and dancing. But I still couldn't believe it. Everyone was running toward the midan. Many were kissing the officers and the soldiers. Some were on top of the tanks to have their pictures taken with the officers. People chanted, "The army and the people are one hand!"

I must listen to the statement myself. I went up to Pierre's flat. They were all congratulating each other. They were all embracing.

"Really?"

"Yes, really!"

"So it did happen?"

"Yes, it did happen!"

I ran to the TV room. All the channels were rebroadcasting the statement that was delivered by Omar Suleiman:

> In the name of God the Merciful, the Compassionate. Citizens, in these very difficult circumstances Egypt is experiencing, President Mohamed Hosni Mubarak has decided to step down from the office of president of the republic and has charged the Supreme Council of the Armed Forces to administer the affairs of the country. May God help everybody.

I called my parents to congratulate them.

"Mabrouk! Congratulations!"

Their voices were joyful just like everybody else's.

We improvised a song, "Leave, leave, please leave," to the same melody as a popular song by Afaf Radi that said, "Please smile." We danced, sang, and jumped like children. Ululations and joy!

Songs were being blasted from all the sound systems in the midan. People were cheering and dancing. Fireworks lit the sky of the midan. We heard something pop and looked inside from the balcony; a young man had just opened a bottle of champagne.

"So you've heard!"

"No. Today is my birthday."

"Really?"

"Yes, really!"

"This is a historic birthday!"

We celebrated with him and drank to his health and the health of the entire Egyptian people.

I opened my Facebook page and posted the news, "He stepped down. We did it in eighteen days. Anyone who wants to depose a president should contact us Egyptians at 00225012011." Instantly, congratulations poured in from friends all over the world. One of the funniest was from a foreign friend who had written, "Uninstalling dictator: Process complete," and had also commented that Mubarak was not even a dictator but a stupid civil servant.

Many friends arrived with huge quantities of all kinds of goodies, chocolate, and cakes. We devoured them all.

There was another statement by the Supreme Council of the Armed Forces, delivered by one of the generals. We listened attentively.

Fellow citizens, at this decisive moment in Egypt's history, marked by President Mohamed Hosni Mubarak's decision to resign from the position of president of the republic and to charge the Supreme Council of the Armed Forces with administering the affairs of the country, we all realize the gravity of this moment in face of the demands of our great people for fundamental change. The Supreme Council of the Armed Forces aspires, with the help of God, to realize the aspirations of our great people. The Supreme Council of the Armed Forces will issue subsequent statements to delineate a roadmap, with clear steps that will be followed.

At the same time, the Council is not a substitute for legitimacy that is determined by the people, and it salutes, with great esteem and respect, President Mohamed Hosni Mubarak for his lifetime of patriotic endeavor, at war and at peace, and for his patriotic decision to uphold the national interests of the homeland.

At this juncture, the Supreme Council of the Armed Forces wishes to salute the souls of the martyrs who sacrificed their lives for the freedom and security of their country, as well as all the members of its great people. May God help us and grant us peace and success.

"Did you notice how heartfelt his salute to the martyrs was?"
"Not like that halfwit who referred to them as 'your martyrs'!"
"But he still saluted Hosni Mubarak."
"It's okay. It's a matter of decency—he was their commander-in-chief, after all."

I must admit that my admiration for the armed forces grew after the general's military salute to the souls of the martyrs. I asked Pierre's permission to take some of the sweets to the officers and soldiers.

"Of course!"

I carried a large tray with an assortment of goodies and went down. I made my way with difficulty in the midst of the crowds and went to Captain Maged Boulos. People were embracing him and having their photo taken with him. I stopped in front of him and smiled. He waved to me.

"Give them to the soldiers first."

I offered the sweets to the soldiers, but they hesitated.

"Give them to those inside the tank. They may be a bit shy."

I went to the other side of the tank.

"Help yourselves, guys. In celebration of the resignation."

They immediately accepted with great and visible joy.

"Me too, I want my picture with you on the tank," I said to Captain Maged, laughing out loud.

"Wait a little, just wait a little until things get quieter. Take a look around you!"

Another raid of kisses and hugs by men, young and old, descended upon Captain Maged, who had come to be known as "the Lion of the Midan." The soldiers laughed as they stood on their tanks, bending over to grab little children in their arms and pose for photos, and bending over once again to deliver them back to their parents. Incredible that their arms were still functioning!

As I headed toward Merit, I embraced everyone on the way, those I knew and those I didn't know. Laughter, sweets, and cold drinks inundated the place. Joy, joy in all of Egypt and possibly in the entire world that had certainly been watching our revolution.

I returned to Talaat Harb Street. The tuk-tuks, our local version of rickshaws, made their way into Downtown, loaded with passengers beyond their capacity and blasting music. I laughed. The scene was quite unbelievable: tuk-tuks in the heart of downtown Cairo on Talaat Harb Street! Young guys had gathered in circles and started to dance. I walked back to Captain Maged.

"Come on, I want a photo with you."

He laughed and asked the soldier to get a chair, so I could climb up to the tank. He went ahead of me. I stood on the chair but the distance to the top of the tank remained difficult for me to climb.

"Give me your hand."

Captain Maged grabbed one hand, and the soldier grabbed the other, as I burst into a fit of laughter.

"Okay, now, go!"

They pulled me up. I stood on top of the tank between them and felt proud. I gave my cell phone to one of the soldiers and showed him how to take a picture.

"How do I get down now? It looks pretty tough!"

"No worries, I'll stand on the chair and bring you down."

Maged stood on the chair and I stood at the edge of the tank. He took my hand and pulled me toward him. We almost locked into an embrace. He began to apologize.

"I'm the one who should apologize."

As soon as I landed safely on the ground I found young Emad waiting for me. He hugged me and congratulated me.

"Congratulations to *you* and your martyred brother."

"Come and dance with me."

"Where?"

"Over there," pointing in the direction of a group dancing around the tuk-tuks.

"Are these guys your crowd?"

"Yeah, they're my relatives and friends."

"And the tuk-tuks?"

"Three of them belong to my relatives and the others belong to friends."

"I can't believe that they all came from Bulaq al-Dakrour in their tuk-tuks!"

"Come on, let's dance."

I followed him to the circle. The young guys began to cheer. I danced with Emad to music I had never heard before.

"What is this music? Where did you guys get this?"

"From Bulaq al-Dakrour!"

We laughed, until our eyes watered. I was very happy for Emad.

I spotted a group of my friends, so I excused myself.

"Where are you guys going?"

"After Eight just opened!"

"Okay, let's go!"

We got to After Eight. Inside everybody was singing: "On my rababa I sing, live on Egypt." Everybody was clapping and sharing drinks.

"No music?"

"Someone went to get a cassette player."

We danced and sang until a friend came back with a big cassette player.

We inserted a cassette and pressed play.

We cheered and sang along.

Pink
My life is pink.
Pink, pink, pink, pink.
My life is pink with you by my side.
I am by your side, my love,
And my love, you are by my side.

The song ended.

"Encore! Encore!"

We changed the lyrics.

Pink, pink
My life is pink without you, Hosni.
Without you Hosni, life is now pink.
Pink, pink, pink.

Modern Arabic Literature

The American University in Cairo Press is the world's leading publisher of Arabic literature in translation.

For a full list of available titles, please go to:

mal.aucpress.com

REVOLUTION
IS MY NAME